The Workbook on the TEN COMMANDMENTS

The Workbook on the TEN
COMMANDMENTS

Maxie Dunnam and
Kimberly Dunnam Reisman

UPPER
ROOM BOOKS®
NASHVILLE

Cover design: Gore Studio, Inc. | www.GoreStudio.com
Cover photo: Corbis Images
First printing: 2004

Library of Congress Cataloging-in-Publication Data

Dunnam, Maxie D.
  The workbook on the Ten commandments / by Maxie Dunnam and Kimberly Dunnam Reisman.
    p. cm.
  ISBN 0-8358-9875-X
  1. Ten commandments. I. Reisman, Kimberly Dunnam, 1960– II. Title.

BV4655.D84 2004
241.5'2—dc22   2003019485

Printed in the United States of America

To

Don and Paula Bourland

Thad and Julie Farrell

Tom and Dee Dyer

David and Millie Gedney

Harold and Dot Goodwin

David and Donna Libby

Tom and Dianne Long

Jack and Betty Moore

Dusty and Trudy Rhodes

dear friends who have encouraged us on our journey

and to

Jean Brindle

Phil Emerson

wonderful colleagues whose nurture and

mentoring have been invaluable.

OTHER BOOKS
BY MAXIE DUNNAM & KIMBERLY DUNNAM REISMAN

The Workbook on the Seven Deadly Sins

The Workbook on Virtues and the Fruit of the Spirit

BY KIMBERLY DUNNAM REISMAN

The Christ-Centered Woman: Finding Balance in a World of Extremes

Knowing God: Making God the Main Thing in My Life

BY MAXIE DUNNAM

The Workbook of Living Prayer (20th Anniversary Edition)

The Workbook on Becoming Alive in Christ

The Workbook on Christians Under Construction and in Recovery

The Workbook on the Christian Walk

The Workbook on Coping as Christians

The Workbook on Intercessory Prayer

The Workbook on Loving the Jesus Way

The Workbook on Spiritual Disciplines

The Workbook on Keeping Company with the Saints

The Workbook on Lessons from the Saints

Contents

Introduction

We find the Ten Commandments in two places: Exodus 20 and Deuteronomy 5. Significantly they were given just after the Israelites were led from slavery out of Egypt, and again, forty years later, just before they would enter the Promised Land. God gave them, written on two tablets, to Moses at Mount Sinai; scripture says the very finger of God wrote them. The first three commandments deal with our relationship with God. The fourth commandment, about the sabbath, bridges us from our relationship with God to our relationships with others. The last six concern our relationships with others, beginning with our family and working out from there; moving from our actions (murder, adultery, theft) to our words (lying by giving false testimony) to our attitudes (that of coveting our neighbors' property). The Ten Commandments were given in the form of covenant—a solemn and binding agreement initiated by God, given to God's people. To keep the covenant is to inherit blessing. To break it is to reap disaster.

The Ten Commandments are the bedrock foundation on which legal systems are built. Throughout the history of the world, great societies have required these ten words to be posted, often by law in public places. During the English Reformation in England, the law required the Ten Commandments, the Lord's Prayer, and the Apostles' Creed to be posted on the walls of public places. The Ten Commandments have always provided the moorings for civilization. Today, though, we live in an age without moorings. In 1997 in Montgomery, Alabama, Judge Roy Moore was ordered to remove the wooden plaques of the Ten Commandments from his courtroom. He challenged the order and lost. It was ruled unconstitutional and a violation of the establishment clause of the First Amendment. Interestingly, Roy Moore later was elected to the Alabama Supreme Court and ordered the Ten Commandments returned to the courtroom. Once again higher courts ordered them removed. All over this land, the Ten Commandments have been removed from courthouse walls, from the walls of jails and prisons, and from other public places. Is it any wonder that less than 1 percent of Christians in America can recite the Ten Commandments from memory?

The century just closed is probably the most brutal, perhaps the cruelest century in the history of the world. Just as the Israelite nation stood at the edge of the Promised Land, we stand on the edge of a new millennium. The answer for renewing the moral fabric of civilization is not as simple as posting the Ten Commandments in our classrooms and courtrooms, though that might help. The answer lies in returning to the Lord our God. Perhaps the most important words of the commandments are in the prologue: "I am the LORD your God, who brought you out of the land of Egypt, out of the house of slavery" (Exod. 20:2). The ten words would call us to remember God's deliverance from the cruel slavery of Egypt and challenge us to return to the Lord our God, who has created and delivered us and who continues to deliver us.

The days are surely coming, says the LORD, when I will make a new covenant with the house of Israel and the house of Judah. It will not be like the covenant that I made with their ancestors when I took them by the hand to bring them out of the land of Egypt—a covenant that they broke, though I was their husband, says the LORD. But this is the covenant that I will make with the house of Israel after those days, says the LORD: I will put my law within them, and I will write it on their hearts; and I will be their God, and they shall be my people (Jer. 31:31-33).

Though Jeremiah could not see how it would happen, he knew it would. Hundreds of years later there was One who came and said, "I am the light of the world"; "I am the bread of life"; "I am the way, and the truth, and the life"; "I am the resurrection and the life." That was his way of saying, "I am the Lord your God." He came to lead us out of our own Egypt—the slavery to sin and death. He came to write his law in our minds and on our hearts. He came to establish a new covenant. Only through Christ can we truly keep the commandments, so this workbook is from a Christian perspective.

One of the most fascinating figures in the New Testament is the rich young ruler who came to Jesus asking, "Good teacher, what must I do to inherit eternal life?" (Luke 18:18, NIV). Matthew, Mark, and Luke tell the story, a haunting story of a person seeking truth, looking for eternal life. He had not found it within the moral and intellectual structures of his faith.

Jesus, a teacher of the law, did what you would expect; he pointed the man to a sure beginning point—the Ten Commandments. The young man had been there and done that. "All these I have kept since I was a boy" (v. 21, NIV). Jesus then summoned the young man to a personal discipleship that transcended cultivation of ethical values, rigid adherence to rules, or scrupulously keeping of the letter of the law. Jesus said, "You still lack one thing. Sell everything you have and give to the poor, and you will have treasure in heaven. Then come, follow me" (v. 22, NIV).

We desire this study to assist in discipleship. We do not regard the Ten Commandments as a burden to bear or a restriction of our freedom but a resource given by God to enable us, under the guidance and power of the Holy Spirit, to follow his Son, Jesus; to make Jesus Lord; and to live out a discipleship that will demonstrate God's reign.

A big issue is how we balance law and freedom, or law and *grace*. We began writing this book in the month following September 11, 2001—the day when terrorists dramatically and deliberately declared war on the United States by sending suicide planes into the Pentagon and the World Trade Center towers. Already restrictions have been instituted, freedom curtailed, rules and regulations added, especially to our travel. A low-key debate has begun, but it will become more intense—in the Congress and in the public arena: How far *can* we or *must* we go in restricting personal human rights? It is a dialogue and debate about law and freedom, how law preserves and guarantees freedom.

Apart from this concern triggered by blatant terrorism, for decades now we have witnessed the increase of lawlessness. Law does not seem to be a deterrent to unbridled expression of violence. We want freedom, but we also long for social stability, intelligent structures, and sensitively controlled patterns for our common life. We know that the rule of law does not guarantee freedom; laws can be tyrannical. We also know—as demonstrated in the best expressions of Western civilization—that law plays a major role in creating a world in which ordinary persons can be free and regard themselves as their own masters. It is a curious and challenging paradox: Only a rule of law, accepted and abided by, can preserve freedom. Thus the importance of the Ten Commandments.

A new day dawned for Israel at Sinai. God's people now had specific expressions to guide them in their covenant relationship with Yahweh. Commandment and covenant were united. We know this was not the first expression of these laws. Precisely where they came from, we're not sure. They have a universal quality, somehow lying buried in the history of humankind but now given unique expression. For Israel, the giving of the law to Moses was the most important event in their history and, they dared to believe, the most important event in the history of the world. However we assess their notion, it is true that in the Ten Commandments, we have guidelines that can be boundaries in which we may have our freedom to move without fear. In God's mercy, God has provided in the Ten Commandments a freedom we can enjoy and limitations that, when abided by, guarantee a mutual freedom for all God's children.

We write from a Christian perspective, believing Jesus' claim: "Do not think that I have come to abolish the law or the prophets; I have come not to abolish but to fulfill" (Matt. 5:17). Jesus probed the essence of God's law, going back behind the law of his day, and summarized the essence of God's law:

> One of the scribes came near and heard them disputing with one another, and seeing that he answered them well, he asked him, "Which commandment is the first of all?" Jesus answered, "The first is, 'Hear, O Israel: the Lord our God, the Lord is one; you shall love the Lord your God with all your heart, and with all your soul, and with all your mind, and with all your strength.' The second is this, 'You shall love your neighbor as yourself.' There is no other commandment greater than these" (Mark 12:28-31).

This summary of the law will flavor our consideration of the Ten Commandments.

HOW TO USE THIS WORKBOOK

This workbook is designed for individual and group use. Let's look at the process, which is simple but important.

The plan for this workbook calls for an eight-week commitment. You are asked to give about thirty minutes each day to reflect on some aspect of the Ten Commandments to inform, enhance, and shape your faith and life. For some persons, the thirty minutes will come at the beginning of the day. However, if it is not possible for you to give the time at the beginning of the day, do it whenever the time is available, but do it regularly. This is not only an intellectual pursuit; it is also a spiritual journey, the purpose of which is to assimilate the content into your daily life. This journey is personal, but our hope is that you will share some of your insights with fellow pilgrims who will meet together once each week during the eight weeks of the study.

The workbook is arranged in eight major divisions, each designed to guide you for one week. These divisions contain seven sections, one for each day of the week. Each day of the week will have three major aspects: (1) reading, (2) reflecting and recording ideas and thoughts about the material and your own understanding and experience, and (3) some practical suggestions for weaving ideas from the reading material into your daily life. Each day's commentary won't be too much to read, but it will be enough to challenge thought and action.

Quotations other than scripture are identified in parentheses at the end of each selection. The citation gives author along with book title and page number, Web site, or audiotape where the quotation may be found. These citations are keyed to the Sources section at the end of the workbook where you will find complete bibliographic information should you wish to explore certain works more fully.

Throughout the workbook you will see the symbol ——∞——. When you come to that symbol, please stop. Do not read any further. Think and reflect as we guide you in order to internalize the ideas shared or the experience reflected upon.

REFLECTING AND RECORDING

After the reading each day, you are asked to record some of your reflections. The degree of meaning you receive from this workbook depends largely on your faithfulness in practicing its method. You may be unable on a particular day to do precisely what is requested. If so, then simply record that fact and make a note of why you can't follow through. This exercise may give you some insight about yourself and help you to grow. On some days there may be more suggestions than you are able to deal with in the time you have available. Do what is most meaningful for you, and do not feel guilty about the rest.

Finally, always remember that this pilgrimage is personal. What you write in your workbook is your private property. You may wish to share it with no one. For this reason no two people should attempt to share the same workbook. The importance of what you write is not what it may mean to someone else but what it means to you. Writing, even if only brief notes or single-word reminders, helps you clarify your feelings and thinking.

The significance of the reflecting and recording dimension will grow as you move along. Even beyond the eight weeks you will find meaning in looking back to what you wrote on a particular day in response to a particular situation.

SHARING THE JOURNEY WITH OTHERS

In the history of Christian spirituality, the spiritual director or guide has been a significant person. To varying degrees, most of us have had spiritual directors—individuals to whom we have turned for support and direction in our spiritual pilgrimage. There is a sense in which this workbook can be a spiritual guide, for you can use it as a private venture without participating in a group. The value of the workbook will be enhanced, however, if you share the adventure with eight to twelve others. (Larger numbers tend to limit individual involvement.) In this way, you should also profit from the growing insights of others, and they will profit from yours. The text includes a guide for group sharing at the end of each week.

If this is a group venture, everyone should begin the workbook on the same day so that when you come together to share as a group, all of you will have been dealing with the same material and will be at the same place in the text. It will be helpful if you have an initial get-acquainted group meeting to launch the adventure. A guide for this meeting is provided in this introduction.

Group sessions for this workbook are designed to last one and one-half hours (with the exception of the initial meeting). Those participating in the group covenant to attend all sessions unless an emergency prevents attendance. There will be eight weekly sessions in addition to this first get-acquainted time.

GROUP LEADER'S TASKS

One person may provide the leadership for the entire eight weeks, or leaders may be assigned from week to week. The leader's tasks are:

1. Read the directions and determine ahead of time how to handle the session. It may not be possible to use all the suggestions for sharing and praying together. Feel free to select those you think will be most meaningful and those for which you have adequate time.

2. Model a style of openness, honesty, and warmth. A leader does not ask anyone to share what he or she is not willing to share. Usually, as leader, be the first to share, especially in the case of personal experiences.

3. Moderate the discussion.

4. Encourage reluctant members to participate and try to prevent a few group members from dominating the conversation.

5. Keep the sharing centered in personal experience rather than academic debate.

6. Honor the time schedule. If it appears necessary to go longer than one and one-half hours, the leader should get consensus for continuing another twenty or thirty minutes.

7. See that the meeting time and place are known by all, especially if meetings are held in different homes.

8. Make sure that the necessary materials for meetings are available and that the meeting room is arranged ahead of time.

It is a good idea to hold weekly meetings in the homes of the participants. (Hosts or hostesses may make sure there are as few interruptions as possible from children, telephones, pets, and so forth.) If the meetings are held in a church, plan for an informal setting. Participants are asked to dress casually, to be comfortable and relaxed.

If you wish to include refreshments, serve them after the formal meeting. In this way, those who want to stay longer for informal discussion may do so, while those who need to keep to the time schedule will be free to leave, having had the full value of the meeting time.

SUGGESTIONS FOR INITIAL GET-ACQUAINTED MEETING

The initial meeting's purpose is getting acquainted and beginning the shared pilgrimage. Here are ideas for getting started:

1. Ask each person in the group to give his or her full name and the name by which each wishes to be called. Address all persons by the first name or nickname. If members need nametags, provide them.

2. Let each person in the group share one of the happiest, most exciting, or most meaningful experiences he or she has had during the past three or four weeks.

3. After this experience of happy sharing, ask any who are willing to share their expectations of this workbook study. Why did they become a part of the group study? What does each expect to gain from this endeavor? What are his or her reservations?

4. Review the introduction to the workbook and ask if there are questions about directions and procedures. (As a leader, you should have read the Introduction prior to the meeting.) If people have not received copies of the workbook, hand out the books now. Remember that everyone must have his or her own workbook.

5. Day 1 in the workbook is the day following this initial meeting, and the next meeting should be held on Day 7 of the first week. If the group must choose a weekly meeting time other than seven days from this initial session, the reading assignment may be adjusted so that the weekly meetings are always on Day 7, and Day 1 is always the day following a weekly meeting.

6. Nothing binds group members together more than praying for one another. Encourage each participant to write the names of all individuals in the group in his or her workbook and commit to praying for them by name daily during the seven weeks.

7. After checking to see that everyone knows the time and place of the next meeting, close with a prayer, thanking God for each person in the group, for the opportunity for growth, and for the possibility of growing through spiritual disciplines.

God bless you as you continue this workbook journey.

NOTE: Though we are writing jointly, there are occasions when a first-person story or experience will be shared without specific identification of the person writing. We believe this style makes reading flow more naturally.

Week One
Foundations

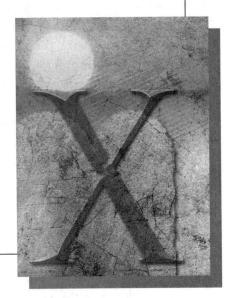

DAY 1

A Stone of Remembrance

Then God spoke all these words: I am the LORD your God, who brought you out of the land of Egypt, out of the house of slavery; you shall have no other gods before me.

You shall not make for yourself an idol, whether in the form of anything that is in heaven above, or that is on the earth beneath, or that is in the water under the earth. You shall not bow down to them or worship them; for I the LORD your God am a jealous God, punishing children for the iniquity of parents, to the third and the fourth generation of those who reject me, but showing steadfast love to the thousandth generation of those who love me and keep my commandments.

You shall not make wrongful use of the name of the LORD your God, for the LORD will not acquit anyone who misuses his name.

Remember the sabbath day, and keep it holy. Six days you shall labor and do all your work. But the seventh day is a sabbath to the LORD your God; you shall not do any work—you, your son or your daughter, your male or female slave, your livestock, or the alien resident in your towns. For in six days the LORD made heaven and earth, the sea, and all that is in them, but rested the seventh day; therefore the LORD blessed the sabbath day and consecrated it.

Honor your father and your mother, so that your days may be long in the land that the LORD your God is giving you.

You shall not murder.

You shall not commit adultery.

You shall not steal.

You shall not bear false witness against your neighbor.

You shall not covet your neighbor's house; you shall not covet your neighbor's wife, or male or female slave, or ox, or donkey, or anything that belongs to your neighbor.—Exodus 20:1-17

During the days of the California gold rush, a young man and his bride set out across the country to make their fortunes. Somewhere along the way they drank contaminated water, and the young bride became ill and died before they could reach Fort Kearney in Nebraska. The young man was heartbroken. He took the body of his bride to the highest hill and buried it, using the wagon bed to make a coffin. Then he drove down some wooden stakes to mark the grave, thinking that he would go on west and later come back. The more he thought about it, the more certain he became that he could not go on. He said to himself, "I'll forget where this is; I will never remember it." He retraced his steps all the way back to Saint Louis, Missouri. He found a stonecutter and had him prepare a tombstone engraved with the name "Susan Hale," along with the date of her birth and death.

He sought to find someone who would haul it back for him, but all the wagons going west were overloaded, and no one would help him. In desperation, but in an inspiring act of commitment, he bought a wheelbarrow, put the stone in it, walked those weary miles back toward Fort Kearney, and set the stone up on her grave.

It's a tender, powerful story. That young man knew that there are some things we must never forget. For him, his bride's grave was a sacred spot on earth, and he must always remember its location. So it is with Mount Sinai and the Ten Commandments. The Ten Commandments have been set up for us so that we will never forget the importance of these eternal truths and values.

You can't miss the fact that the laws are in the form of absolutes: "You shall" or "You shall not." A more common expression of law was conditional: "If you do this or that, then I will do this or that." Today we do not easily affirm absolutes. A typical response to a moral consideration is, "Yes, I did it—but it's not all that bad."

- I lied, but no one knew the truth, so it's not all that bad.
- Sex with someone else's wife? We were kindred spirits, so it's not all that bad.
- Honesty—on my income tax? Who knows how much I earned and how I spent what I earned? I work hard for my money. It's not all that bad.
- Personal rights and privacy—it's my choice. I fear I am unable to support a child financially; I feel emotionally ill-equipped to rear a child with no paternal participation. Abortion? It's not all that bad.

We redefine morality on the basis of preference because we're not willing to live by absolutes.

The Ten Commandments originally represented the claims of God upon a comparatively barbarous people—a people whose morality had been corrupted by habitual contact over several generations with the vices of a heathen state. Superstition and idolatry had degraded their religious thought. These laws were given to the human race at almost its lowest and weakest condition. If we fail to seek to keep these basic, elementary rules of life, how shall we regard the other precepts and guides for living that have come to us through Christ and his teaching?

These commandments can never become obsolete because they belong to God's revelation of God's self, God's character, will, and relationship with humankind. The changing circumstances of the human race cannot destroy the significance and worth of these "absolutes"; nor can we define morality apart from our consideration of them. The truth is, God claims authority over our moral life. God claimed that authority in the earliest times; God claims it still.

REFLECTING AND RECORDING

Think back to your first encounter with the Ten Commandments. How did you first start hearing about them? Can you remember the first time you saw a plaque or a parchment on which the commandments were printed? Who first talked to you about the Ten Commandments?

———— ✤ ————

*(Remember, whenever you see this symbol, stop and
follow the instructions for reflecting before you go on in the text.)*

Without referring to your Bible or the beginning text for today, write in your own words as many of the Ten Commandments as you can. Next, number them in order of their importance as you perceive it.

Spend four or five minutes simply reflecting on the place the Ten Commandments have had in your life as you have sought to grow in your relationship with God.

DURING THE DAY

On page 167 there is a copy of the Ten Commandments, briefly stated. Cut out the Ten Commandments. Carry them with you today and throughout this week. Every chance you get, take them out and read them. If you have not already memorized them, this is the beginning of that process. Seek to memorize the commandments by the end of this week.

DAY 2
Gradual Brimstone

Then the LORD said, "How great is the outcry against Sodom and Gomorrah and how very grave their sin! I must go down and see whether they have done altogether according to the outcry that has come to me; and if not, I will know."

So the men turned from there, and went toward Sodom, while Abraham remained standing before the LORD. Then Abraham came near and said, "Will you indeed sweep away the righteous with the wicked? Suppose there are fifty righteous within the city; will you then sweep away the place and not forgive it for the fifty righteous who are in it? Far be it from you to do such a thing, to slay the righteous with the wicked, so that the righteous fare as the wicked! Far be that from you! Shall not the Judge of all the earth do what is just?" And the LORD said, "If I find at Sodom fifty righteous in the city, I will forgive the whole place for their sake." Abraham answered, "Let me take it upon myself to speak to the Lord, I who am but dust and ashes. Suppose five of the fifty righteous are lacking? Will you destroy the whole city for lack of five?" And he said, "I will not destroy it if I find forty-five there." Again he spoke to

him, "Suppose forty are found there." He answered, "For the sake of forty I will not do it." Then he said, "Oh do not let the Lord be angry if I speak. Suppose thirty are found there." He answered, "I will not do it, if I find thirty there." He said, "Let me take it upon myself to speak to the Lord. Suppose twenty are found there." He answered, "For the sake of twenty I will not destroy it." Then he said, "Oh do not let the Lord be angry if I speak just once more. Suppose ten are found there." He answered, "For the sake of ten I will not destroy it." And the LORD went his way, when he had finished speaking to Abraham; and Abraham returned to his place.
—Genesis 18:20-33

*T*he audacity of Abraham to negotiate with God about the destruction of Sodom and Gomorrah! Here we find one of the dramatic and memorable stories of the Old Testament. Only recently did one line in that story attract our attention. "Then the LORD said, 'How great is the outcry against Sodom and Gomorrah and how very grave their sin! I must go down and see whether they have done altogether according to the outcry that has come to me; and if not, I will know'" (vv. 20-21).

God seems amazed. Was God surprised that sin had advanced to such a state?

Calvin Miller, one of the most imaginative preachers today, used this text in a sermon he titled "Gradual Brimstone." In it he said,

> I used to think that outside the city of Gomorrah was a huge billboard that said, "The wickedest city in the world—depravity is us." But knowing the human race's uncanny ability of self-congratulation, I suspect the Gomorrahans saw themselves as moral, normal people. I have in my life, after all, known only a few wicked people, and they never thought so.

Miller then imagined that when God said to Abraham, "I'm going to rain down burning sulphur on these cities," Abraham replied,

> "Whatever for, God? I mean, Gomorrah is 39 percent born again, and 64 percent of the people there attend some church or synagogue at least once a month. Why are you going to do that?"
> God said, "Because they're wicked."
> Abraham said, "You mean wicked like the Wicked Witch of the East in Oz?"
> "Yes, except that Gomorrah is not in Kansas," said God. "Furthermore, it looks pretty rotten to me."

Calvin Miller concluded, "I think God was saying that brimstone is never all at once . . . it is gradual. It is always a case of the amphibian in the stewpot. If you warm it gently, the creature is cooked and can't remember" (Miller, *Preaching Today* audiotape 214).

Yesterday we considered the fact that one characteristic of the Ten Commandments is that they are absolute, not conditional, and that they are expressed in the second-person singular form. The King James Version reads, "*Thou* shalt not," preserving the singular form distinctly, which the modern translation *You* does not. To be sure, this singular pronoun may be interpreted as speaking to Israel as a community, but we need to heed this emphatic reminder, a probing call to each individual within the community to bear responsibility to the law and to obey it.

REFLECTING AND RECORDING

Yesterday you were asked to reflect on how the Ten Commandments have expressed themselves in your life, how they have shaped your relationship with God. Continue reflecting in that fashion, but focus on this: Recall a time in your life when these Ten Commandments were more rigidly adhered to than now. To what degree are you abiding by these commandments?

———◦◦◦◦———

Describe how these commandments are relevant to our day and the ways they have specific application for you.

Recall the last time you had a conversation with someone about the role of individual morality in our culture and how we as a people, corporately, may have lost our sense of sin. Make some notes about the occasion and the key points in that conversation.

DURING THE DAY

As often as possible, continue to read the Ten Commandments that you are carrying with you. Seek to memorize these by the end of the week. Observe any situation where you sense that one of the Ten Commandments is being violated.

DAY 3
The Trumpet in the Morning

An old story relates that sometime after the devil rebelled against God and was cast out of heaven, he was asked what he missed most from his life in heaven. The devil thought for a moment then replied, "I miss most the sound of the trumpet in the morning." What the devil did he mean? The "sound of the trumpet" had a role in the giving of the Ten Commandments.

When all the people witnessed the thunder and lightning, the sound of the trumpet, and the mountain smoking, they were afraid and trembled and stood at a distance, and said to Moses, "You speak to us, and we will listen; but do not let God speak to us, or we will die." Moses said to the people, "Do not be afraid; for God has come only to test you and to put the fear of him upon you so that you do not sin." Then the people stood at a distance, while Moses drew near to the thick darkness where God was (Exod. 20:18-21).

It's a dramatic story: thunder and lightning, the mountain engulfed in smoke, and out of that awesome sight and sound a trumpet blared, and the people trembled with fear. They welcomed any word from Moses, but they thought God's speaking meant death. Moses calmed their fears, assuring them that God desired to keep them from sinning. In the Ten Commandments, God spoke—like the sound of a trumpet—not only to the Hebrew people but to all humankind, offering a way in which to walk.

Paul, in his first letter to the Corinthians, made the case for people to speak clearly and understandably: "Even in the case of lifeless things that make sounds, such as the flute or harp, how will anyone know what tune is being played unless there is a distinction in the notes? Again, if the trumpet does not sound a clear call, who will get ready for battle?" (1 Cor. 14:7-8, NIV).

God is not a judge seated on the throne in heaven but a parent teaching children to walk.

When Paul described the resurrection and eternal life, he used the sound of the trumpet: "Listen, I tell you a mystery: We will not all sleep, but we will all be changed—in a flash, in the twinkling of an eye, at the last trumpet. For the trumpet will sound, the dead will be raised imperishable, and we will be changed" (1 Cor. 15:51-52, NIV).

In legend, at least, even the devil knows the importance of the sound of the trumpet. The Ten Commandments provide the sound of the trumpet. Here is a law by which we are to abide and a way in which we are to walk.

The Ten Commandments remind us that there are eternal laws in the universe by which we must live if life is going to come out God's way. The issues addressed are acts that are wrong, not just because the Ten Commandments say so. God said they were wrong because the moral law of the universe won't support killing and stealing and committing adultery.

The word *law* may be misleading if it gives the impression of God handing down laws that must be minutely observed on pain of death or suggests God as an implacable legislator who seeks to inhibit us from what we enjoy. In the original Hebrew the word *law* does not suggest that at all. It means "to teach." So our vision of God is not a judge seated on the throne in heaven but a parent teaching children to walk, telling them how to avoid dangers, helping them understand the nature of relationship between children and parents and children with one another. The prophet Hosea provides a wonderful such picture when he reports God saying, "When Israel was a child, I loved him, and out of Egypt I called my son" (Hos. 11:1).

REFLECTING AND RECORDING

Name in your mind two or three persons who have played a role in teaching you the way you are to live. Spend a few minutes reflecting on how the Ten Commandments influenced their lives and how they taught you.

Recall and record briefly here an occasion when someone confronted you with the fact that you had broken one of the Ten Commandments. It may have been one of your parents, a teacher, a family member, a close friend. Get the details of that in your memory and make some notes about it here.

How do you most often perceive God: as a lawgiver who demands that you keep the law or as a parent who guides and teaches? Why?

DURING THE DAY

Continue to memorize the Ten Commandments. Continue to observe in your daily relationships and activities occasions when one of the Ten Commandments may be broken.

DAY 4
Keeping It Precious

Here, O Israel: The LORD is our God, the LORD alone. You shall love the LORD your God with all your heart, and with all your soul, and with all your might. Keep these words that I am commanding you today in your heart. Recite them to your children and talk about them when you are at home and when you are away, when you lie down and when you rise. Bind them as a sign on your hand, fix them as an emblem on your forehead, and write them on the door-posts of your house and on your gates.—Deuteronomy 6:4-9

I recently used Laurie Beth Jones's book *Jesus in Blue Jeans: A Practical Guide to Everyday Spirituality* during my morning devotional time. One morning her focus was "keeping it precious." She began by asserting that almost every commandment God gave to Moses was designed to keep it precious—meaning to keep life precious. What a tremendous thought.

So often in our culture we think God is trying to hem us in: *Don't do this! That's not allowed!* We can even feel God is playing games with us, that the commandments are some kind of cruel joke, a set of rules God invented, knowing we'd never be able to follow them.

Our culture places a premium on self-fulfillment, equating self-fulfillment with experiencing as much as possible. The message is that new and different experiences, or "extreme" experiences are the way to self-fulfillment. In that type of environment, it is easy to wonder if God is holding out on us. What is it that God is trying to keep us from experiencing? Why all the prohibitions?

But as with so much of our culture today, focus is skewed. It is not a multitude of experiences that leads to fulfillment; it is deep and lasting relationships, with God and others, that provide true meaning for our lives. That is what Laurie Beth Jones is referring to when she says that God is trying to "keep it precious." When God said to Moses, "Do not worship any other gods," God was keeping the divine-human relationship precious. Jones writes:

> Remember the sabbath—Keep this day precious.
> Honor your father and mother—Keep them precious.
> Thou shalt not kill—Keep life precious.
> Thou shalt not commit adultery—Keep the marriage vows precious.
> Every commandment instructing us not to lie, cheat, or steal is
> really about keeping truth, honor, and respect for God and one another
> precious (Jones, *Jesus in Blue Jeans*, 98).

Many of the problems we experience in life are the result of our not keeping it precious. God has given us holy things—our bodies, minds, hearts, mouths, eyes—and rather than keeping them precious, we have undervalued them, often even misusing and abusing them. It is no wonder our society is drowning in crimes of hatred, neglect, and violence. As Jones says, "We have become the pigs trampling pearls" (Jones, *Jesus in Blue Jeans*, 99).

REFLECTING AND RECORDING

Return to the quote by Laurie Beth Jones about how each commandment keeps it precious. Considering each claim, in what ways do you agree with her? How might this understanding of the commandments shape your understanding of and your keeping of them?

———— ∞ ————

Spend four or five minutes reflecting on this assertion: Many problems we experience in life are the result of our not keeping it precious. Record ways you have found this true in your own life.

DURING THE DAY

Continue memorizing the Ten Commandments. As you move through this day, see if you can identify an occasion, relationship, or action that broke one of the Ten Commandments and resulted when a person did not "keep it precious."

DAY 5
Not to Earn God's Love

There is therefore now no condemnation for those who are in Christ Jesus. For the law of the Spirit of life in Christ Jesus has set you free from the law of sin and of death. For God has done what the law, weakened by the flesh, could not do: by sending his own Son in the likeness of sinful flesh, and to deal with sin, he condemned sin in the flesh, so that the just requirement of the law might be fulfilled in us, who walk not according to the flesh but according to the Spirit.—Romans 8:1-4

Our worship team gathers on Tuesdays to design the upcoming Sunday service as well as to plan ahead. A while back we undertook a series on the Ten Commandments. As we discussed how to approach this series, our first question was much like what we explored yesterday: Why did God give us the commandments? Many opinions were expressed. Some individuals felt that God gave us the commandments to show how we would have to perform in order to earn God's love. Others offered the suggestion that the purpose was to set us apart, to make us a unique people, intimately connected to God and others. Another person suggested God gave us the commandments as a way to assure that we would live well.

The more we have pondered the question, the more we realize that while there may be many opinions regarding why God gave us the commandments, there's only one thing we can know with absolute certainty: The commandments were not given as the means through which we work our way toward God. We can never do that successfully. We will never be able to do enough good or avoid enough bad to earn God's love. The violence in our world tells us that on a massive and overwhelming level. Our daily experience tells us that on a subtler, more intimate level as well. There are consequences to our actions that we never intended. We accidentally hurt when we try to help. Our sense of self-preservation surfaces as we lash out at someone even though we know we shouldn't. These unintended consequences remind us that in our own power, we will never be able to follow as God desires.

The scripture passage above reminds us of the good news: We do not have to earn God's love. We do not have to raise ourselves to God's level. God has come to us through Jesus Christ and has made a way for us. No matter what we believe about why God gave us the commandments, this much is true: Keeping them is not a way to earn God's love; we have God's love already. Liberation from earning God's love through our behavior does not let us off the hook however. God gave the commandments intending for us to follow them, and there are good reasons to do so.

REFLECTING AND RECORDING

On Day 3 you considered whether you envision God as a lawgiver or as a parent who wishes to teach you. Keeping that in mind, ponder this statement: The commandments were not given as a means to work our way toward God; we are to remember that God loves us first.

Look at your own experience with persons whom you love and care about. Is your relationship with any of them dependent upon your keeping certain rules or acting a certain way? Do these relationships and the conditions surrounding those relationships influence your perception of God and God's relationship with you?

Recall and record briefly here an occasion when you violated a commandment, disobeyed a parent, or refused to keep a condition of relationship with a loved one, and yet that parent or loved one accepted you and loved you despite what you had done.

Return to your reflection on your understanding and perception of God. Put that understanding and perception up against these statements: God's love is not dependent upon our behavior. God's forgiveness is always available when we fail. God's love remains constant.

Spend a few minutes reflecting on this statement: God gave us the commandments because God desires that we live well.

DURING THE DAY

Continue reading and memorizing the Ten Commandments. Continue the observation you began yesterday: Look for occasions when breaking any of the Ten Commandments was a failure to keep it precious.

DAY 6
Law and Grace

The question of law and grace is usually raised when we consider the Ten Commandments. Usually behind our thinking lies the question: *Are Christians required to keep the Ten Commandments?* Debating whether to keep the Ten Commandments does not settle the issue of grace. Yes, Christians are to keep the Ten Commandments, and this does not put law above grace. Though we are saved by grace and are not dependent upon works, the spirit of the Ten Commandments is binding on us all. Jesus said that he did not come to abolish the law but to fulfill it (Matt. 5:17). On one occasion, in two statements Jesus summarized not only the manner in which the Old Testament law should be kept but also the impact of the Prophets: "'You shall love the Lord your God with all your heart, and with all your soul, and with all your mind.' This is the greatest and first commandment. And a second is like it: 'You shall love your neighbor as yourself.' On these two commandments hang all the law and the prophets" (Matt. 22:37-40).

In the New Testament, obedience evidences love for the Lord. The fact that we're under grace instead of the Old Testament legal relationship with God should not lead us to think that the Ten Commandments do not apply to us. Grace gives us freedom and joy in being obedient. Since we know that keeping the law perfectly is not the basis for our salvation, we can live boldly in our obedience, knowing that when we stumble over the law, or because of the law, or in keeping the law, our salvation is still intact because of grace.

Grace gives us freedom and joy in being obedient.

In a sense, keeping the law is "the narrow gate" through which we must enter if we're to find life. Jesus expressed it this way: "Enter through the narrow gate; for the gate is wide and the road is easy that leads to destruction, and there are many who take it. For the gate is narrow and the road is hard that leads to life, and there are few who find it" (Matt. 7:13-14).

We can't have everything in life; therefore, to have the important things demands the ability to discriminate, to discipline ourselves. As we grow in our relationship with God and as we mature in our Christian discipleship, we discover certain values and relationships that are not to be compromised and never to be surrendered.

A bank president was having an affair with a female employee, and this created all sorts of problems for the bank. The board of directors hired a psychologist to consult with them and to offer advice about the situation. After two hours of discussion, they asked the psychologist to give his opinion. He said, "Tell him to stop it."

The board members were stunned with the simple answer. They had paid this fellow good money, and this was all the advice he was offering?

They called the president into the meeting and simply told him to stop the affair.

An interesting thing happened. The president was more than willing to abide by the decision.

Deep down, we know that whenever we are doing wrong, or intend to do something wrong, the solution is to simply stop it (Dunnam, *Perceptions,* 93).

One of our heroes, Bishop Gerald Kennedy, had a marvelous commentary on the paradox of narrowness and broadness: "The man who will not make up his mind but dabbles in every interesting possibility is the man whose very wideness makes him shallow. If it is necessary to be broad enough to escape narrowness, it is also necessary to be narrow enough to be deep" (Kennedy, *The Lion and the Lamb,* 143).

REFLECTING AND RECORDING

List what you could never compromise or surrender, e.g., a faithful relationship with your spouse.

Recall and record briefly, perhaps in notes only you can understand, an occasion when you did compromise a value or a relationship. Note the pain, estrangement, negative fallout, or destructiveness that may have resulted.

Can you think of a person who fits the observation "Every person has a price"? Write that person's first name; then briefly record what that person did that was a compromise, a surprising violation of value, or a surrender of convictions that causes you to think that he or she had a price.

DURING THE DAY

Continue memorizing the Ten Commandments. Continue the observation you began on Day 4: Look for occasions when breaking a commandment resulted in failing to keep it precious.

DAY 7
The Mount to Which We Can Come

The Hebrew people had seen a great sight in which no other people have shared. As they stood massed on the level plain at the foot of Mount Sinai, they beheld the upheavals of nature when God was present. In the Exodus account the people are filled with dread; they were panic-stricken, thinking that they would die. Moses sought to calm their fears: "Do not be afraid; for God has come only to test you and to put the fear of him upon you so that you do not sin" (Exod. 20:20). That helped a bit. The people stood at a distance, "while Moses drew near to the thick darkness where God was" (v. 21). There is a lesson here for us as we begin to live intimately with the Ten Commandments. Not unlike the Hebrew people, we're glad to participate in God's merciful providence and to believe that God will guide and provide for us. But we draw back, trembling at the thought of God involved in every aspect of our life. Or we are guilty of "keeping God on the mountain," giving to a "Moses" the task of standing between us and God: our priest or pastor, our creed, our stained-glass illumined places of worship, a sacrament. "You speak to us, and we will listen; but do not let God speak to us, or we will die" (v. 19). The epistle to the Hebrews provides needed perspective.

> You have not come to something that can be touched, a blazing fire, and darkness, and gloom, and a tempest, and the sound of a trumpet, and a voice whose words made the hearers beg that not another word be spoken to them. . . . But you have come to Mount Zion and to the city of the living God, the heavenly Jerusalem, and to innumerable angels in festal gathering, and to the assembly of the firstborn who are enrolled in heaven, and to God the judge of all, and to the spirits of the righteous made perfect, and to Jesus, the mediator of a new covenant, and to the sprinkled blood that speaks a better word than the blood of Abel (Heb. 12:18-24).

Let's seek to settle this now—in our minds and hearts: As Christians, we move toward welcoming God's life and light into the innermost recesses of our souls; toward yielding to Christ the key to every department of our lives, allowing God's hand to guide and provide benevolent providence; toward believing that even the hairs on our heads are numbered by a God who loves us, who has come to us in Jesus Christ and has made a new covenant with us.

REFLECTING AND RECORDING

Here are the Ten Commandments you have memorized this week:

____ You shall have no other gods before me. ____

____ You shall not make for yourself an idol. ____

____ You shall not take the name of the Lord your God in vain. ____

____ Remember the sabbath day and keep it holy. ____

____ Honor your father and mother. ____

____ You shall not murder. ____

____ You shall not commit adultery. ____

____ You shall not steal. ____

____ You shall not bear false witness. ____

____ You shall not covet. ____

On the left side of these commandments put a check (✓) by those that are most difficult for you to keep—ones you perhaps have violated most often. Now, on the right side of the commandments, put a check by any one of them that you have not violated in the past two months.

Write a brief prayer committing yourself to a serious consideration of the Ten Commandments during this workbook study, a commitment to welcome God's life and light into the innermost recesses of your soul, to yield to Christ as much of your life as you presently understand, a commitment to allow God to guide your mind and heart in the weeks ahead.

DURING THE DAY

Since this is the seventh day of your first week, if you are a part of a group, you will be meeting with those persons. Pray for them as you move through this day, and pray that the group's sharing will benefit all the persons who will come together.

If you are not a part of a group, call someone you know and love and tell him or her that you are doing this study of the Ten Commandments and invite that person to pray for you as you move through this experience.

Group Meeting for Week One

Leader: You will need a chalkboard or newsprint for this session and an instant camera, if one is available. If an instant camera is not available, bring a regular one.

INTRODUCTION

Group sessions are most meaningful when all participants share their experiences. This guide is designed simply to facilitate personal sharing. You need not be rigid in following these suggestions. The leader especially needs to be sensitive to what is happening in participants' lives and focus the group's sharing of those experiences in light of that knowledge. Ideas are important; we need to wrestle with new ideas as well as with ideas with which we disagree. It is important, however, that the group meeting not become a debate. Emphasize individuals—their experiences, feelings, and meaning. Content is important, but applying content to our individual lives and to our relationship with God and others is more important.

As group members come to the point where all can share honestly and openly what is happening in their lives, group meetings will be more meaningful. This does not mean that group members share only the good or positive; they can also share their struggles, difficulties, and negatives.

This process of group sharing is not easy; it is deceptive to pretend otherwise. Growth requires effort. Don't be afraid to share your questions, reservations, and "dry periods" as well as meaningful times.

SHARING TOGETHER

1. Begin your time together by allowing all persons to share memories of their first encounters with the Ten Commandments: How did you first hear of the Ten Commandments? Can you remember where you first saw them written or displayed in a public place? Who was the first person to talk to you about the Ten Commandments? It is helpful for the leader to begin the sharing.

2. Invite two people to take two or three minutes to reflect on the place of the Ten Commandments in their lives as they have sought to grow in relation to God.

3. On Day 4 we considered Laurie Beth Jones's claim that God's commandments were designed to help us "keep it precious." Sabbath, marriage, life, parents—all are to be kept precious. Spend five to eight minutes talking about this function of the Ten Commandments.

4. Using a chalkboard or newsprint, record the responses of the group to this question: Why do we or should we keep the Ten Commandments?

5. Discuss this list of reasons in light of the three reasons given on Day 5: (1) to show that we are connected with God; (2) not to earn God's love but to show gratitude for that love; (3) because God wants us to live well and has given us guidelines to promote wholeness.

6. Invite two or three people to share briefly recollections of an occasion when someone confronted them with the fact that they had broken one of the Ten Commandments.

7. How do persons respond to the claim "There is no freedom without law"? Spend five to eight minutes discussing this.

8. Spend the remaining time talking about law and grace. Do the two conflict with each other? How can we balance law and grace? How can a loving God make such bold commandments?

PRAYING TOGETHER

Each week's suggestions call for the group to pray together. Corporate prayer, one of the great blessings of Christian community, empowers Christians, so including this dimension in a shared pilgrimage is important.

Group members need to feel comfortable during corporate prayer. No one should feel pressured to pray aloud. Silent corporate prayer may be as vital and meaningful as spoken corporate prayer. God does not need to hear our words spoken aloud to hear our prayers. Times of silence, when thinking is centered and attention is focused, may foster our deepest prayer.

Verbalizing thoughts and feelings to God in the presence of fellow pilgrims can also be a powerful experience for a community on a common journey. Verbal prayers may be offered spontaneously as persons choose to pray aloud. Avoid suggesting, "Let's go around the circle now, and each one pray."

Suggestions are given each week for this "praying together" time. The leader for the week should regard these only as suggestions. What is happening in the meeting—the mood, the needs expressed, the timing—determines the direction of the group's prayer time together. Here are some possibilities for this closing period.

1. Invite the group to spend a few minutes in silence, deliberately thinking about each person in the group and what that person has shared. Offer a silent sentence prayer of petition or thanksgiving for that person.

2. Invite any two or three persons to offer a brief, spontaneous prayer, thanking God for the group and the opportunity to share with others in this study/learning/prayer experience.

3. With the instant camera, take a picture of each person. (If you do not have an instant camera, use whatever camera is available, get pictures developed during the week, and do this exercise at your next gathering.) Turn pictures facedown on the table and ask each person to choose one. (If someone picks his or her own picture, let that person select another one.) Ask group members to pray during the coming week for the person in their picture. Encourage each individual to talk to the person whose picture he or she selected and ask about concerns or events that could be incorporated into prayer. Remind group members to bring the photos back next week.

4. Here's an alternative to the option in number 3. Everyone writes the names of group members in the front of their workbooks. Each person then prays for all group members during the week. Participants will be amazed at their receptivity to one another during times of sharing once they have prayed for their group companions daily.

Week Two

No Other God

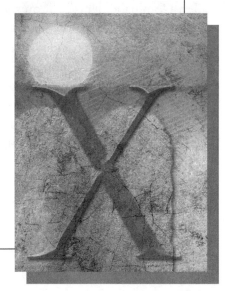

DAY 1
What We Believe Matters

What we believe matters. How many times have you heard, "It doesn't matter what you believe as long as you are sincere"? In this age when pluralism has become an ultimate virtue, how prevalent is the attitude "One religion is as good as another since all religions lead to God"!

We are writing in the aftermath of September 11, 2001. That day etched horror in our minds. The pictures will remain vivid for a long time: raging fires, smoke and debris darkening the sky, huge buildings aflame and collapsing, screaming persons fleeing for their lives, courageous police and firefighters risking their lives to save others, 188 persons dead from the Pentagon crash, over 2,700 buried beneath the crushed stone and twisted steel of the World Trade Center, the lives of 261 passengers and crew on the four planes snuffed out.

We knew before sunset on September 11 that indeed it does matter what people believe. In a sermon the Sunday following this infamous day, Dr. George Hunter, professor at Asbury Theological Seminary, voiced what had been made unmistakably clear: "It's bad theology that has created a small constellation of very narrow, dogmatic, totalitarian governments. It's bad theology that causes them to oppress their own girls and women at a rate we can scarcely imagine. And it's bad theology that shapes their irrational passion to demolish the entirety of Western culture. What you believe matters so much that if they believed in a different kind of God, they would be different people."

The first words in the Bible are, "In the beginning God. . . ." (Gen. 1:1, NIV). The first of the Ten Commandments is, "You shall have no other gods before me" (Exod. 20:3). Just as the Bible begins history with God, so it begins the law with God.

As history has unfolded, people's belief about God has passed through three stages: polytheism, henotheism, and monotheism. We'll give specific consideration to these tomorrow. For now, register the fact that the final stage is monotheism, the belief that there are not many gods; nor is there a god for each nation as henotheism holds; rather, there is only one God for all the earth.

It certainly matters what we believe about the one God. "If people believe in gods at all, they will necessarily wish to be like the gods in whom they believe, and therefore, the kinds of gods they believe in will make all the difference to the kind of life which they live" (Barclay, *The Ten Commandments*, 16). What we believe matters: We must get the idea of God right, for inevitably we will become like the god we worship.

REFLECTING AND RECORDING

On Day 3 last week, we contrasted the notions of God as a judge seated on a throne in heaven and as a parent teaching children to walk. Make a list of images of God you recall from scripture or from teaching—for instance, creator, judge, father, mother.

_____   _____
_____   _____
_____   _____
_____   _____
_____   _____
_____   _____
_____   _____

Put a check (✓) beside the images that you most often use or connect with God. Next, go over the list and put a plus (+) beside the images that you feel harmonize most with God's giving of the Ten Commandments. If you put a plus (+) by an image that you did not check (✓), ponder why you do not connect that image with God in your understanding and experience.

Spend the balance of your reflection time thinking about persons and situations that confirm the fact that what you believe matters.

DURING THE DAY

Seek to have a conversation with someone today on the theme "What you believe matters."

   If you are a part of a group using this workbook, design a plan to pray each day for the members of your group.

DAY 2
God Who Is One and All

Yesterday we introduced the fact that people's belief in God passed through three stages: polytheism, henotheism, and monotheism. William Barclay summarized these stages well. In the first stage, *polytheism*, people believed in many gods. While this belief is no longer very common, at the time of the Israelites people did believe in a multitude of gods—a god of the sun, a god of the moon, of the sea, of fire, of the wind, of the river, of the sky, and on and on almost endlessly. The world was crammed with gods and goddesses who competed, as it were, for the gifts and the worship of humankind.

In the second stage, *henotheism*, a nation would restrict its worship to one god, and the worship of any other god would be prohibited. This didn't mean that other gods did not exist—in fact, everyone accepted the fact that they did—but a nation had its own god and would worship no other. Thus gods and goddesses were supreme within their own territory.

An interesting development would occur when a ruler of one nation married a prince or princess from another nation. That prince or princess would bring his or her own gods and more often than not, another god would be added to the nation's worship. In 1 Kings 11:1-8 we see this happening with King Solomon. According to scripture, the Lord became angry with Solomon because his heart had turned away from "the God of Israel" (v. 9).

The final stage of belief about god is *monotheism*—the belief that there is not simply one god for each nation but there is one God for all the earth. The Jews believe in one God and thus we have the first commandment. The Revised Standard Version gives this commandment in two forms: "You shall have no other gods before me"; then, in the margin, this rendition: "You shall have no other gods besides me." William Barclay reminds us about henotheism, in which Yahweh was the God for Israel, while there were other gods for other nations, and monotheism, the belief that there is no god but Yahweh. Throughout the Old Testament we find numerous references to other gods and to "our God" as the greatest of these. The God story unfolds slowly in scripture as the people come to understand that the God among many gods is the God who is One and the God who is All.

Another characteristic of the Hebrew understanding of God is that God belongs to a people rather than a place. The chief difference between the God of Abraham, Isaac, and Jacob, and the gods of other tribes, is that God loves God's people. Unlike other gods, El Shaddai (one of the names for God) does not stand apart from the people. Yet God is so awesome, so righteous and holy, so beyond human knowledge and understanding, that the Jews refuse to speak God's name. Though God belongs to a people, not a place, God cannot be domesticated. Madeleine L'Engle has aptly observed that there is "a wish in some professional religion-mongers to make God possible, to make [God] comprehensible to the naked intellect, domesticate [God] so that [God's] easy to believe in" (L'Engle, *Glimpses of Grace*, 2).

L'Engle goes on to observe: "Every century the Church makes a fresh attempt to make Christianity acceptable. But an acceptable Christianity is not Christian; a comprehensible God is no more than an idol" (L'Engle, *Glimpses of Grace*, 2).

REFLECTING AND RECORDING

Thinking about your own belief, is there any hint of polytheism or henotheism in your understanding of God? What about the understanding of people you know? Describe your thoughts. Do you know anyone who would be polytheistic? henotheistic?

Spend two or three minutes reflecting on this assertion: We will become like the gods we worship.

———— ✧ ————

In the third stanza of the popular hymn "Holy, Holy, Holy! Lord God Almighty" we find a clear affirmation of monotheism: "Only thou art holy; there is none beside thee." Let the awesome splendor of these words settle in your mind.

> Holy, holy, holy!
> Though the darkness hide thee,
> though the eye of sinful man thy glory may not see,
> only thou art holy;
> there is none beside thee,
> perfect in power, in love and purity (*The United Methodist Hymnal*, #64).

———— ✧ ————

Spend some time pondering L'Engle's conviction that "a comprehensible God is no more than an idol." Is this a more dogmatic assertion of the hymn's words "though the darkness hide thee, though the eye of sinful man thy glory may not see"? Make notes of your thoughts.

What does it mean to say "an acceptable Christianity is not Christian"?

DURING THE DAY

Seek to engage someone in a conversation around the theme "a comprehensible God is no more than an idol."

Have you designed a plan to pray for members of your group sharing this workbook journey? Do so and pray daily for them.

DAY 3
Reluctance in Our Relationship with God

O LORD, you have searched me and known me./You know when I sit down and when I rise up;/you discern my thoughts from far away./You search out my path and my lying down,/and are acquainted with all my ways./Even before a word is on my tongue,/O LORD, you know it completely./You hem me in, behind and before,/and lay your hand upon me./Such knowledge is too wonderful for me;/it is so high that I cannot attain it.—Psalm 139:1-6

On Day 7 last week, we considered our dread of being in God's presence—the way we want a "Moses" to stand between us and God. We're quite happy to worship God in the heavens above but are unwilling to entertain the possibility of our earth crowned with the presence of God and every bush aflame with divine fire. F. B. Meyer identifies three causes for reluctance in our relationship with God. (1) We're in danger of mistaking the true intention of our existence. (2) We are deeply conscious of our sinnership. (3) A belief lurks in the heart of humanity that we are more merciful than God (Meyer, *Devotional Commentary on Exodus*, 238-341). Let's look at these.

We are in danger of mistaking the true intention of our existence. For this were we born—for this came we into the world that we might live, move, and have our being in God. Beyond that we are to *know* that we are living in that manner.

What the water is to the fish, what air is to the bird, what sunshine is to the eagle, that God's nature was intended to be to ours. As well might the fish ask not to be thrown into the water, or the bird ask that its cage-door might not be opened, admitting it to the air, or the eagle fly into a darksome cage away from the glorious sunlight, as that any [person] should say, "Let God not speak to me lest I die." The exact contrary is true: If God does not speak to us, we shall die; for the Speech of God is Jesus Christ, THE WORD (Meyer, *Devotional Commentary on Exodus*, 239).

Test yourself. How long has it been since you consciously thought that you came from God?

———❦———

• that you need God, that you are akin to God?

———❦———

• that you have been made in God's image and after God's likeness?

———❦———

- that you are known completely by God?

- that there is no way to flee from God's presence?

- that you can never be truly at rest until you rest in God?

- that God's "hand will guide me, [God's] right hand will hold me fast" (Ps. 139:10, NIV)?

Our second reluctance in our relationship with God, in Meyer's words, is that *we're deeply conscious of our sinnership*. If you are Christian, you know that the more you grow in your relationship with the Lord, the more sensitive you are to your sin and failure. All along the way, you recognize the fact that there is no one who has not missed the mark. Even as Christians, this awareness can produce reluctance to move deeper in our faith.

What about those who are not yet Christian, who make no conscious affirmation of seeking God? Does their awareness of their *sinnership* drive them passionately to seek diversion? They seem desperate for immunity from themselves, unable to be alone, always seeking experiences that divert their thoughts from themselves. They are, as Jesus describes, people who "hate the light and do not come to the light" (John 3:20). They seem to avoid anything that reminds them of God.

Meyer describes the third reluctance for a relationship with God as *a lurking belief in our hearts that we are more merciful than God*. Most of us are unaware of this dynamic. Yet if we examine ourselves, we can identify its subtle influence in our lives since it is tied to our awareness of sinnership. Certainly, knowing our sinfulness, God became flesh to manifest the fullness of God's nature and passionate desire for our redemption, as the epistle to the Hebrews tells us:

> Therefore he had to become like his brothers and sisters in every respect, so that he might be a merciful and faithful high priest in the service of God, to make a sacrifice of atonement for the sins of the people (Heb. 2:17).

REFLECTING AND RECORDING

Do you have any reluctance in your relationship with God? Do any of Meyer's three causes for reluctance fit you?

Recall and describe an experience in which you felt your loved ones and friends were being more merciful than God.

Recall occasions in your life when you sought to keep God at a distance because you were so aware of your sin and felt guilty and ashamed. Describe that experience here.

How have the two experiences you have recalled shaped your present understanding and experience of God?

DURING THE DAY

A portion of the psalmist's prayer is printed on page 167. Cut it out and put it in a place where you can see it during the day—on the sun visor of your car, bathroom mirror, refrigerator door. Make it your prayer for the balance of the week.

 DAY 4
Me, an Atheist?

*M*y friend was baffled and surprised that I would be so dogmatic and plainspoken. There was also a sigh of pain as he winced at my statement: "That sounds like atheism to me." His words expressed his shock: "Me, an atheist?"

We had been talking about his faith journey and where he was in his relationship with Christ. Maybe he expressed it a bit more strongly than he actually believed, and maybe he wanted to show me how "liberal" he was—how inclusive and tolerant. I don't know whether he had thought much about what he was saying. I have heard his sentiments so often—unexamined sentiments for most people, politically correct and seldom challenged in the context of the pluralism prevalent in too much of the Christian community. I was more direct than I usually am and I fairly blurted it out—"sounds like atheism to me."

I was responding primarily to his statement "It doesn't matter so much what someone believes, so long as that person lives a good life." He had been making other statements, such as, "Every person has a right to believe as he or she pleases"; and, "I don't care what you believe as long as you are sincere."

Maybe I responded so immediately and directly because I had been spending a lot of time with the Ten Commandments. When I made that response, I was thinking of the first and second commandments.

> You shall have no other gods before me. You shall not make for yourself an idol, whether in the form of anything that is in heaven above, or that is on the earth beneath, or that is in the water under the earth. You shall not bow down to them or worship them; for I the LORD your God am a jealous God, punishing children for the iniquity of parents, to the third and the fourth generation of those who reject me, but showing steadfast love to the thousandth generation of those who love me and keep my commandments (Exod. 20:3-6).

Nothing tentative about that. Nothing ambiguous. It is a command: "You shall have no other gods before me. You shall not make for yourself an idol." Walter Brueggemann, the eminent Old Testament scholar, says *command* is the "defining and characteristic marking" of the true God (Brueggemann, *Theology of the Old Testament*, 182). Accepting that truth, Stanley M. Hauerwas and William H. Willimon add that "the most striking characteristic of communication between God and Israel is that of command-obedience" (Hauerwas and Willimon, *The Truth About God*, 26).

My friend's shrug-of-the-shoulders "it doesn't matter what one believes" description of where he was in relation to God couldn't go unchallenged. When I told him it sounded like *atheism*, I had to do some explaining. I was not talking about a classically defined atheism: There is no God. I can't remember when I last talked to a person who didn't believe there is a god. But *practical atheism* is common, even among us Christians. We believe in God but live as though God doesn't matter. We affirm our faith in "God, the Father, the Almighty, Maker of heaven and earth," but we do not see that affirmation of faith as a "characteristic marking" of our lives. The creed that we corporately attest in community worship hardly defines who we uniquely are.

The issue, then, is not belief but obedience. Atheism is not a biblical matter. The Bible does not deal with whether or not there is a God; rather, the paramount issues are who God is and what God is like. So the first and second commandments make it clear that our relationship with God is the foundation of our entire lives. This relationship affects everything else. For better or worse, what we believe about who God is, how we relate to God, and how we experience God relating to us determine our interaction with other people and with the rest of the world.

We believe in God but live as though God doesn't matter.

Submission to any authority is a quaint notion in our modern culture. We are so bound to our own egos that any suggestion of obedience or submission is considered authoritarian and unfair for "liberated" persons. We have become *servants of self*. Though we boast of our freedom from external authority, our servitude to self is a destructive bondage. Slavery comes in many guises:

- the insatiable drive for pleasure that makes idols of sex and money
- the relentless passion for security
- the desire to "fit in" which makes us victims of advertising's definition of the good life.

The question is not whether we are going to live under a "master" with external commands. The question is: Which master and which external commands do we choose?

REFLECTING AND RECORDING

Reflect on the suggestion that taking the position "it doesn't matter what one believes" is an expression of practical atheism.

———— ✺ ————

To what degree are you a practical atheist, believing in God but living as though God doesn't exist?

———— ✺ ————

Write a brief paragraph about what you believe obedience and submission to God mean.

DURING THE DAY

Continue your use of the prayer from Psalm 139.

DAY 5
The God Who Delivers

We continue today thinking about obedience. Do you notice that the strongest argument for obedience is the experience of past deliverance? God says, as a prelude to the commandments, "I am the LORD your God, who brought you out of the land of Egypt, out of the house of slavery" (Exod. 20:2). Certainly that should ring a bell when we think of our own deliverance.

Many of us know the story of Millard Fuller, the founder of Habitat for Humanity. Millard got on the fast track pursuing material wealth even while in college. He became a millionaire as a young man, but his pursuit of wealth—he would say his enslavement to that pursuit—almost destroyed his marriage. In desperation, he and his wife, Linda, sought to put the relationship together again. God intervened in a remarkable way; Millard surrendered his wealth and yielded himself completely to the Lord. In a dramatic move, he and his wife decided to give away their money and pursue a different lifestyle. This decision led to the founding of Habitat for Humanity, a ministry that makes homeownership a reality for the working poor. In the past twenty-five years, over 125,000 houses have been built, and 100,000 more are planned for the next five years.

When Millard shares his testimony, he doesn't hesitate to use the word *deliverance*. He was delivered from enslavement to materialism, to money, to security. That's the story of God's activity in our lives, for our God is the One who brought each one of us "out of the house of slavery."

God is a personal God, available to meet our needs. Scripture is filled with that witness. "I called to the LORD out of my distress, and he answered me" (Jon. 2:2). "My God will fully satisfy

NO OTHER GOD   35

every need of yours according to his riches in glory in Christ Jesus" (Phil. 4:19). "Even though I walk through the darkest valley, I fear no evil; for you are with me." (Ps. 23:4). "Do not be afraid, little flock, for it is your Father's good pleasure to give you the kingdom" (Luke 12:32).

The first commandment declares that at the very center of our lives must be enthroned a living God. For us Christians, at the center of life must be one God, who became human in Jesus Christ. As indicated yesterday, if a person has many lords, then he or she is in bondage to all of them. If there are many lords in our lives, then we are confused by their conflicting claims; we will always live in disharmony; a civil war will rage within. But when we yield ourselves to God, we are released from other captivity.

We are to know and acknowledge God as the One who has delivered us, and as the first word of the Bible says, as the One who created us. So the commandment is: Know me! Acknowledge me! Remember me! I am the Lord your God. This first commandment is affirmed in a remarkable sentence, the heart of the Torah for the Jew: "Hear, O Israel: The LORD our God, the LORD is One" (Deut. 6:4, NIV). The Jews call this the Shema, and it is the word most often on their lips in worship. To that description of God is added the word "Love the LORD your God with all your heart and with all your soul and with all your strength" (Deut. 6:5, NIV).

REFLECTING AND RECORDING

Recall and record here what you consider your most explicit or radical act of obedience to God.

Did your obedience have anything to do with experiencing God as One who delivers? If so, reflect on that deliverance experience.

———— ⌘ ————

Make some brief notes about how you experience, or have experienced, Jehovah as "God that is, God that will be, and God that was" in the following:

Our present—"God that is."

Our Past—"God that was."

Our Future—"God that will be."

DURING THE DAY

Continue to use the prayer from Psalm 139.

Try to identify experiences today that will confirm Jehovah's presence *now, in the past*, and *in the future*.

DAY 6
Freedom in Bondage

*I*n a sense, this first commandment is the greatest because it provides the motivating power for all the rest. The remaining commandments mean little or nothing unless commitment to God generates a compelling desire to obey God. Few, if any, readers would confess to breaking this commandment. For that reason, we need to remember Martin Luther's word, "Whatever thy heart clings to and relies upon, that is properly thy God." Our children, our spouse, our home, security, position, power, social prestige, love of family, love of country, profession, job—it is not uncommon for any of these to replace God as our first commitment. Jesus put the matter plainly. On one occasion the Pharisees got together to confront Jesus.

> One of them, a lawyer, asked him a question to test him. "Teacher, which commandment in the law is the greatest?" He said to him, "'You shall love the Lord your God with all your heart, and with all your soul, and with all your mind.' This is the greatest and first command- ment. And a second is like it: 'You shall love your neighbor as yourself.' On these two com- mandments hang all the law and the prophets" (Matt. 22:35-40).

With this summary of the law, Jesus told us how to live: "But strive first for the kingdom of God and his righteousness, and all these things will be given to you as well" (Matt. 6:33). We have noted the negative expression of the commandments, the restrictiveness and the apparent removal of some of the pleasure from life. Think more of the other side of this commandment. To be sure, it is a commandment: "You shall have no thing or no one before me," God says. But, "I am your God." That's the other side.

Vernard Eller, a professor of religion, has written one of the most intriguing books on the Ten Commandments, *The MAD Morality, or The Ten Commandments Revisited*. He makes the case that **MAD** magazine with its outlandish humor and satire provides a real commentary on the Ten Commandments. Not intentionally, and certainly not explicitly, **MAD** magazine sees, "with the Ten Commandments, that there are many vaunted freedoms which in fact lead to slavery" (Eller, **MAD** *Morality*, 9).

Eller makes the case that free persons become free and stay free by steering clear of false free- doms. The prelude, God's introduction to the Ten Commandments, is perhaps the most impor- tant word of all: "I am the LORD your God, who brought you out of Egypt, out of the house of slavery" (Exod. 20:2). Eller offers this imaginary conversation between God and Israel:

"Fine! Then let old Yahweh give you a few helpful tips on how to be free men and stay that way, OK?

"You people don't know it, but you stand in danger of losing your new freedom. No, it is not that the Egyptians are about to repossess you; I took good care of them. But in the first place, there are a lot of other gods around here who would dearly love to have you sign on with them. They will make you big promises about the freedoms they have to offer. But be careful! I've already proved that I am the God of Freedom, right?"

"Right!"

"What these gods offer as freedom always turns out to be slavery—that's why they are false gods. One God frees men; any other god enslaves men—that's the difference between the true God and false gods. Therefore . . . you free men shall have no other gods besides me, right?"

"Right!" (Eller, **MAD** *Morality*, 8).

The commandments mark off areas where free persons are not to go; precisely they must not go there if they are going to remain free. That means that there is freedom in bondage. The commandments are guarantees of freedom. Jesus was clear about this. "Enter through the narrow gate; for the gate is wide and the road is easy that leads to destruction, and there are many who take it. For the gate is narrow and the road is hard that leads to life, and there are few who find it" (Matt. 7:13-14).

A negative command certainly prohibits particular actions, but it does so to free us for other actions. Eller argues that if the Ten Commandments correctly spot the threats to human freedom, then their negative expression actually invites persons to find freely whatever lifestyle suits them—as long as they avoid the pitfalls that would destroy their freedom altogether.

Consider a *positive* command, such as: You shall always leave a school building through a red painted door. Over against that put the negative command: You shall not leave school buildings through red painted doors. Which command frees more kids to get out of more school buildings more of the time? Obviously, a negative command can prohibit one action, precisely in order to free one for a host of others, whereas the positive requirement can force one into a given course of action and deny . . . the possibility of all others (Eller, **MAD** *Morality*, 8).

Reflecting and Recording

Identify an area in your life in which you experience freedom because you have been willing to "keep particular laws" or abide by some restrictions. Briefly describe that connection between law and freedom.

Spend a few minutes reflecting on Luther's assertion: "Whatever thy heart clings to and relies upon, that is properly thy God."

The following are common things our hearts cling to. Look carefully at these. Put a check (✓) beside those that tempt you to cling too tightly.

___ Children	___ Social prestige
___ Spouse	___ Love of family
___ Home	___ Love of country
___ Security	___ Profession
___ Position	___ Job
___ Power	

Write a brief prayer confessing either the temptations or the fact that your heart clings to these things you checked. Name them in your prayer. Ask God to forgive you and release you from clinging so tightly to these that they threaten your relationship with God.

DURING THE DAY

Continue to use the prayer from Psalm 139. Pay attention to the little ways you are in bondage to what your heart clings to and relies upon.

DAY 7
The Starting Point—Life with God

The Ten Commandments began where life has to begin—with God. In your reflecting and recording time on the first day of this venture, Day 1 of Week 1, you were asked to arrange the Ten Commandments in order of their importance as you perceive them. We have no idea how you did that, but typically when people do this exercise, they reverse the biblical order. More times than not, they give priority to the commandments dealing with moral and ethical matters, such as stealing, killing, and committing adultery. The commands about our relationship with God usually fall at the end of the list.

This order reflects the widely held definition of Christianity as ethical and moral idealism. The Christian is seen primarily as a moralist. High morals and ethical standards are important if we are going to have a good society. It is important that we do not kill or steal or lie or commit adultery. But these conditions are not to be fulfilled merely because persons are told that this should be the case. There must be a reason behind these prohibitions, and there must be the potential for our keeping the commandments. Consequently, the commandments about our relationship with God come first and must be kept first. God, the source of life, has made known the nature of life, which God has created. Not only so, God has come into this life in the person of Jesus Christ to provide us the capacity for fulfilling the life to which God calls us.

Before giving the Ten Commandments, God instructed Moses:

> Thus you shall say to the house of Jacob, and tell the Israelites: You have seen what I did to the Egyptians, and how I bore you on eagles' wings and brought you to myself. Now therefore, if you obey my voice and keep my covenant, you shall be my treasured possession out of all the peoples. Indeed, the whole earth is mine, but you shall be for me a priestly kingdom and a holy nation. These are the words that you shall speak to the Israelites (Exod. 19:3-6).

It is as though God is saying to Israel, "I paid a high price for you. I brought you out of slavery, not only in order to free you from that bondage, but in order that you might more fully belong to me, and that you might worship me." The word *therefore* in this text is important. As a people, the Israelites have been saved by God; therefore, God owns them as God's treasured possession, and they are to be "a priestly kingdom and a holy nation."

The first commandment comes first because it defines what our worship is going to be. We are not going to have idols. We are not going to kill or steal. We are not going to have sex with other people's spouses. Does that sound strange as a way of defining worship? In that day—as in ours—there were gods of war and sex and gold. But God wants a holy people, people who are set apart for the sake of the world, people who are priests—interceding, making sacrifices, mediating on behalf of others. We have been given a vocation—called, claimed, owned by God in order that we might proclaim God's salvation for all humankind through our speech and actions. In his first epistle, Peter made this clear when he claimed that by the grace of God, even Gentiles had been included in Israel's vocation to be "a chosen people, a royal priesthood, a holy nation, a people belonging to God" (1 Pet. 1:9, NIV). When we worship by keeping the Ten Commandments, we are proclaiming the true God, and we are also showing forth to the world the kind of people God is able to produce.

The commandments about our relationship with God come first and must be kept first.

REFLECTING AND RECORDING

Turn to your Reflecting and Recording on Day 1 of Week 1. How did you order the commandments? Does your recording reflect a more pronounced emphasis on your moral and ethical relationships with others than your relationship with God? Spend a few minutes reflecting on the meaning of how you ordered the commandments.

Describe the difference for you between keeping the commandments because you belong to God and keeping them simply because you know they are moral and ethical demands.

Spend a few minutes reflecting on how your life needs to change if you accept the following statements as true:

- God wants a holy people, people who are set apart for the sake of the world, people who are priests—interceding, making sacrifices, mediating on behalf of others.
- We have been given a vocation—called, claimed, owned by God in order that we might speak and act in a way that proclaims God's salvation for all humankind.
- When we worship by keeping the Ten Commandments, we are proclaiming the true God, and we are also showing forth to the world the kind of people God is able to produce.

If you are a part of a group using this workbook, the group should be meeting sometime today. Look back over this week and make some notes about questions or issues you'd like the group to talk about. Note these questions or issues here.

During the Day

Pray that your group gathering today will be a source of insight, direction, support, and encouragement for all members.

If you are not a member of a group, find a person with whom you feel comfortable sharing and talk about the three statements you considered.

Group Meeting for Week Two

Leader: You will need a chalkboard or newsprint for this session.

INTRODUCTION

Participation in a group such as the one studying this book involves a covenant relationship. You will profit most in your daily use of this workbook if you faithfully attend these weekly meetings. Do not feel guilty if you have to miss a day in the workbook or be discouraged if you cannot give the full thirty minutes in daily discipline. Don't hesitate to share that with the group. We learn something about ourselves when we share our thoughts and feelings with others. You may discover, for instance, that you are subconsciously afraid of dealing with the content of a particular day because its requirements might reveal something about you. Be patient with yourself, and always be open to what God may be seeking to teach you.

Your spiritual growth, in part, hinges upon your group participation, so share as openly and honestly as you can and listen to what others are saying. If you are attentive, you may pick up meaning beyond the surface of their words. Being a sensitive participant in this fashion is crucial. Responding immediately to the feelings you discern is also important. The group may need to focus its entire attention upon a particular individual at times. If some need or concern is expressed, the leader may ask the group to enter into a brief period of special prayer. But participants should not depend solely upon the leader for this kind of sensitivity. Even if you are not the leader, don't hesitate to ask the group to join you in special prayer. This praying may be silent, or a group member may lead the group in prayer. We learned from E. Stanley Jones that whenever Christians come together for sharing, everyone is a teacher and everyone is a learner.

Remember that you have a contribution to make to the group. Even if you consider your thoughts or experiences trivial or unimportant, they may be exactly what another person needs to hear. You need not seek to be profound but simply to share your experience. Also, if you happen to say something that is not well received or is misunderstood, don't be defensive or critical of yourself or others. Don't get diverted by overly scrutinizing your words and actions. Saint Francis de Sales says that "it is self-love which makes us anxious to know whether what we have said or done is approved or not" (Order of Mercy, trans., *A Year with the Saints,* 209).

SHARING TOGETHER

Leader: It may not be possible in your time frame to use all the suggestions provided each week. Select what will be most beneficial to the group. Be thoroughly familiar with these suggestions so that you can move through them selectively, according to the direction in which the group is moving and within the time available. Plan ahead, but do not hesitate to change your plan in response to the sharing taking place and the needs that emerge.

1. To open your time together, the leader may offer a brief prayer of thanksgiving for the opportunity to share with the group and may ask for openness in sharing loving responses with one another.

2. Begin your time together by allowing time for two or three persons to share their most meaningful day of the workbook this week. Why was that day meaningful?

3. Now invite two or three persons to share their most difficult day with the material, describing what they experienced and why it was so difficult.

4. Invite persons in the group to share their images of God from their Reflecting and Recording on Day 1. Write these images on a chalkboard or newsprint. Whenever a person names an image already recorded, put a check (✓) by that image. Now spend six to eight minutes discussing these images. Which are the most popular? Which connect most with your understanding and experience of God? What difference does our belief about God make?

5. Ask a couple of persons to share their reflections on the assertion "We will become like the gods we worship."

6. On Day 3 persons were asked to identify experiences when loved ones and friends seemed more merciful than God, and occasions when they kept God at a distance because of guilt and shame from their awareness of sin. Invite two or three people to share how such experiences affected or shaped their understanding of God.

7. Ask a volunteer to read the paragraph they wrote on Day 4 about the meaning of obedience and submission to God.

8. Give two or three persons the opportunity to share what they consider their most explicit or radical act of obedience to God.

9. Spend eight to ten minutes talking about Luther's word: "Whatever thy heart clings to and relies upon, that is properly thy God."

10. Spend whatever time you have left discussing the three affirmations in the Reflecting and Recording of Day 7.

PRAYING TOGETHER

1. Praying corporately each week is a special ministry. Begin the time of prayer with a period of guided reflection and expression. The leader may say:

   "Let us reflect on those affirmations—if anyone would like to voice a one- or two-sentence prayer in response, please do so."

   After each affirmation, the leader will pause for thirty seconds to a minute for silent reflection or voiced response.

"Let us reflect on these affirmations:

"We have been made in God's image, after God's likeness.

"God knows us completely, and there is no place we can flee from God's presence.

"We need God, and we can never rest until we rest in God.

"There is a place in God's heart that only each of us can fill."

2. Now allow each person to mention any special needs he or she wishes to share with the entire group. A good pattern is to ask for a period of prayer after each need is mentioned. The entire group may pray silently, or someone may offer a brief two- or three-sentence spoken prayer.

3. Close your time by praying together the great prayer of the church, the Lord's Prayer. As you pray this prayer, remember that the prayer links your group with Christians of all time in universal praise, confession, thanksgiving, and intercession.

4. Before you leave, place photos facedown on a table so that each person can receive and pray for a "new" person this week.

Week Three

Making a God
and Trying to Use God

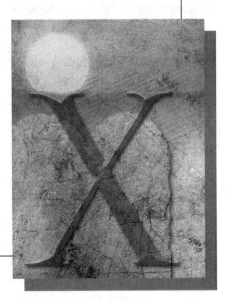

DAY 1
No Idols

You shall not make for yourself an idol, whether in the form of anything that is in heaven above, or that is on the earth beneath, or that is in the water under the earth. You shall not bow down to them or worship them; for I the LORD your God am a jealous God, punishing children for the iniquity of parents, to the third and the fourth generation of those who reject me, but showing steadfast love to the thousandth generation of those who love me and keep my commandments.—Exodus 20:4-6

Can you imagine the scene when the commandments were first given? A motley group of ragtag slaves who have recently been freed from bondage in Egypt stand at the foot of Mount Sinai. The mountain smokes as though on fire. The mountain trembles as though an earthquake moves it. A loud trumpet blast pierces the people's ears, but not as much as the first and second commands pierce their souls: "You shall have no other gods before me. You shall not make for yourself an idol."

The Ten Commandments have not always appeared in the Bible in the form and the order in which they appear today. The present form may have been completed during the Babylonian exile. For the Jewish people the first commandment is not, "You shall have no other gods before me" but the verse "I am the LORD your God, who brought you out of the land of Egypt, out of the house of slavery." The second commandment for the Jewish people is a combination of what Protestants call the first and second commandments. Lutherans and Roman Catholics also combine the first two commandments into one as in the Protestant tradition. Thus the first commandment is, "You shall have no other gods before me. You shall not make for yourself an idol." The close affinity between the first and second commandments obviously emphasizes the call for undivided allegiance, total commitment.

We noted earlier that the first four commandments concern our relationship with God, while the next six commandments concern our relationship with others. The first four commandments, plus the introductory word by which God identifies God's self, provide a marvelous framework for our understanding of God and the relationship that we are to have with God.

There can be no substitutes. The first commandment forbids the worship of any but the true God. The second forbids the worship of any representation of the true God. The Hebrews are forbidden not only to worship any other god but to worship the true God in the wrong way.

The casual reader may conclude that these people would know very little about idols. That is not the case. Review the story of their ancestors, and you will soon come upon story after story of people turning to and treasuring idols. For example, consider the story of Jacob and Laban and their argument over Jacob's wanting to strike out on his own. As a precaution, Jacob's wife Rachel, daughter of Laban, steals her father's household gods while he is away, and she and Jacob begin their journey to freedom. Biblical writers often make fun of idols, and they do so in this story. When Laban catches up with the refugees, he is more interested in recovering his idols than anything else. He searches the caravan and tents but finds nothing. Rachel has hidden them in her camel's saddle. When Laban enters Rachel's tent, he finds her sitting on the saddle. She pleads "the way of women" as her reason for not getting up to greet him. Laban is outwitted. Best of all, the idol is powerless to cry out for help (Gen. 31).

These recently freed slaves had seen idols in Egypt too. Brilliant representations of the sun god Ra must have impressed them. That they remember the idols of Egypt is recorded in the story of their impatience with Moses, who had climbed the mountain to talk to that invisible God. They convince Aaron, brother of Moses, to make them a golden calf and throw a great festival for the occasion.

In commenting on the dramatic sin of idolatry, the making of the golden calf, which will soon happen in Israel at the foot of Mount Sinai where this commandment was given, F. B. Meyer said,

> Had any one suggested that Israel should apostatise from the God of Abraham, they would have stoned him to death. They had no desire to break the first commandment and to have other gods than Jehovah; but they found the demand of the second commandment too vigorous. They must have an image, a visible representation, an idol (Meyer, *Devotional Commentary on Exodus*, 423–24).

Whenever anyone or anything usurps the place that God should have in our lives, we are guilty of idolatry.

Thus they made a golden calf. They had to have a visible image, something they could see and touch. The human heart naturally desires something perceptible by the senses as the object of religious worship. Idolatry is this endeavor to realize by the senses and intellect that which can be apprehended only spiritually.

On the surface there is nothing wrong with having reminders of God or representations of God. These may aid worship for many of us. God is unseen, a spirit and a power invisible to our eyes. So we need symbols, settings, places of worship to be vivid reminders of God.

We have a lot of symbols in our homes and in our studies: crosses, icons, and other beautiful works of Christian art collected from around the world. We have paintings that represent the work of God in the world and the life and ministry of Christ. Before none of these do we bow down and worship. We do not make them idols.

There are actually two prohibitions in this second commandment. First, God bans the making of idols: "You shall not make for yourself an idol, whether in the form of anything that is in heaven above, or that is on the earth beneath, or that is in the water under the earth." That is rather comprehensive, isn't it? "Above the earth, on the earth, or in the waters beneath the earth." Nothing from anywhere in the universe can be used as an idol—nothing that has been created can represent the Creator.

Here is the second prohibition regarding idols: "You shall not bow down to them or worship them." It's one thing to make an idol; it's another to worship it. The problem comes when the symbol, the reminder, becomes a substitute, when it becomes an idol and takes the place of God. In this commandment, God says that we must not represent the Creator by anything created, and we must not render to anything or anyone that which rightly and exclusively belongs to God. The core lesson is this: Whenever anyone or anything usurps the place God should hold in our lives, we are guilty of idolatry.

REFLECTING AND RECORDING

I never will forget my first experience of Buddhist temples in Thailand. In temple after temple, I saw people praying and burning incense to various local gods. Have you ever seen a person actually worshiping an idol? Make notes of any such occasions.

Recall anything in "Christian" worship that may have felt like "idol worship." Make some notes.

What in your home could possibly be considered an idol?

———— ✸ ————

What is the difference, in your experience, between something that reminds us to worship God and an idol?

———— ✸ ————

Spend some time reflecting on this claim: Whenever anyone or anything usurps the place that God should have in our lives, we are guilty of idolatry.

———— ✸ ————

DURING THE DAY

Pay attention today to "idols" you may see on TV, in newspapers, in advertising, in the action and attitudes of people.

DAY 2
Adoration and Worship Belong Only to God

I have a young friend on the verge of self-destruction because he has made an idol of a business project. This young man, a recovering addict, has had a marvelous transformation and has been an ardent Christian—worshiping God, serving and witnessing for Christ, growing in discipleship. In the past few months, a business deal has consumed him. He has grown lax in worship and sabbath observance. His morning quiet time no longer has priority. His attention to his marriage has diminished, and he is in danger of falling back into his old addiction. He would not acknowledge it, but he is breaking the second commandment. His business venture has usurped the place God should have in his life. Though we may not recognize it, all of us have a hierarchy of values. Whatever tops that hierarchy is the god we serve. What our hearts cling to, that to which we entrust ourselves, is our god.

Jesus did not say much about idolatry, but what he said was scathingly clear:

> Do not store up for yourselves treasures on earth, where moth and rust consume and where thieves break in and steal; but store up for yourselves treasures in heaven, where neither moth nor rust consumes and where thieves do not break in and steal. For where your treasure is, there your heart will be also. . . . No one can serve two masters; for a slave will either hate the one and love the other, or be devoted to the one and despise the other. You cannot serve God and wealth (Matt. 6:19-24).

We can make a god out of almost anything: sex, money, security, position, power, family, cars, houses, styles, clothing. When one of these, or anything other than God, is at the apex of our hierarchy of values, we are idolatrous. Whenever we pay ultimate homage to any finite reality, we commit idolatry. As destructive as these forms of idolatry are, they are the fruit of a core idolatry: our failure to trust the only God who can be trusted, the One who gives us the command "You shall have no other gods before me."

Our refusal to trust this One denies God and leads to a search for meaning and salvation in other places. It also leads us to believe that we are sufficient unto ourselves. While the Decalogue is *law*, it is God's gift to Israel, and through Israel to us, to teach us that we cannot go "on our own steam." We cannot make it by our own wits. All of life is gift, God's gift. To forget this or to block this dynamic from shaping our lives courts disaster. We thus remove ourselves from the stream of God's grace and put ourselves into the stream of God's judgment.

Our source of meaning is not autonomy and self-sufficiency but acknowledging ourselves as children of a gracious God whom we can trust and who empowers us to live in trust with others, "to act justly and to love mercy and to walk humbly with [our] God" (Mic. 6:8, NIV).

I have a pastoral relationship with the young man described above. Speaking the truth in love, I confronted him with what I saw as a destructive pattern in his life. Not long after that, the young man called to acknowledge his predicament. He was repentant, confessing that he had relegated God to a secondary place in his life, that he had made his "deal" his god. There was a sadness about him, a broken spirit, but he also showed a confidence and a joy, because he felt he was "on track." Later, he called again. He wanted to talk about the mercy of God. This young man knows that our sin itself is punishment; failing to be who we were created to be constitutes our most painful experience.

REFLECTING AND RECORDING

Take a look at your friends and acquaintances. If there is one among them who, like my young friend, has made or is on the verge of creating an idol, make some notes about your observations.

Make a list of six or eight things you value most. Write them down as they come to mind.

Now number these in sequence according to your order of values.

Reflect on whether God is at the apex of your value system, whether any of these values vie with God for your "worship" and commitment.

DURING THE DAY

"What our hearts cling to, that to which we entrust ourselves, is our god." Take this word with you throughout the day to test yourself about idols.

DAY 3
Idolatry

I couldn't believe it. I was surfing the channels of television sort of mindlessly, looking for a program worth thirty minutes of my time. I came to *The O'Reilly Factor*, a FOX Channel talk show. There was Greta Van Susteren, one of my favorite television personalities. What I couldn't believe was her looks. I could tell it was she, but the dramatic change in her appearance shocked me. O'Reilly interviewed her about why she had had plastic surgery, changing her entire appearance.

Van Susteren emerged as a public television figure during the O. J. Simpson trial. Bright and articulate, she rose rapidly to a place of television prominence. In fact, she had commanded such a strong following on CNN that she was enticed to join FOX. Robin Gerber, a senior fellow at the Academy of Leadership at the University of Maryland, was even more shocked than I at Van Susteren's transformation revealed on her new show, *On the Record*, which debuted on February 4, 2002. Gerber wrote an article for *USA Today* titled, "Why Turn Brilliant Lawyer into Barbie with Brains?" She began with this question: "What do smart, articulate, no-nonsense women do as they break through the glass ceiling of their profession?" Her answer was, "If television talk-show host Greta Van Susteren is any indication, they change their faces."

> Van Susteren is a reminder of the minimalization of American women by American culture. Women are reduced to the sum of our visible parts. We don't need Afghan-style *burqas* to disappear as women. We disappear in reverse—by revamping and revealing our bodies to meet externally imposed visions of female beauty. What you see is not what women have got, but it's first in importance. . . .
>
> Before her surgery, Van Susteren had been an increasingly visible beacon projecting the hope that women had made progress. . . . Now she has become a painful reminder of women's inequality. . . . By trying to become just another pretty face, Van Susteren instead became another cultural casualty" (Gerber, in *USA Today*, February 11, 2002, 17A).

Gerber comments that Van Susteren "is the latest high-profile example of a low-profile cultural truth: How women look is more important than how they think." Van Susteren's act also reflects a culture that puts a glass ceiling above women and demands more of them than men in achieving leadership positions.

More often than not, idolatry relates not to things that are bad but to good things that become overly important to us. Stuart Briscoe makes a confession:

> At one stage in my career it looked as if my preaching days were over. Although I had been at it for many years, tremendous new opportunities had begun to open before me. I stood right on the edge when I suffered an illness that threatened to stop it all. For the only time I can remember I suffered depression. I did not feel at all happy with the situation. My concern, I told myself, stemmed from the fact that I loved to preach about the Lord Jesus. Then in my own heart God spoke to me powerfully, saying, "Stuart Briscoe, do you love preaching about the Lord Jesus more than you love the Lord Jesus about whom you preach?" The answer was yes. I knew I felt upset with the Lord because I could not preach about him. If I had been excited about *him*, it would not have mattered whether I could have preached about him. I felt as if the Spirit of God had said, "You get things in perspective, and you will preach again. Until you get it in perspective, you'll never preach" (Briscoe, *The Ten Commandments*, 27).

When something good becomes overly important to us, we hold it as a possession; it begins to dominate who we are and how we respond to things. It is easy—and it is common—for us to get so excited about what we are doing or what is ours that we worship ourselves and things rather than the Lord. We can turn a good thing into an idol.

Idolatry means that we place ourselves in control rather than God. We trust ourselves more than we trust God. Isaiah confronted Israel with this kind of idolatry. He reminded the Hebrews of how the Babylonians—who had captured them—were burdened down by their idols. He said, "The images that are carried about are burdensome, a burden for the weary. They stoop and bow down together; unable to rescue the burden, they themselves go off into captivity" (Isa. 46:1-2, NIV). Then he speaks directly to the Israelites:

> Listen to me, O house of Jacob,/all the remnant of the house of Israel,/who have been borne by me from your birth,/carried from the womb; even to your old age I am he,/even when you turn gray I will carry you./I have made, and I will bear;/I will carry and will save.
>
> To whom will you liken me and make me equal,/and compare me, as though we were alike?/Those who lavish gold from the purse,/and weigh out silver in the scales—/they hire a goldsmith, who makes it into a god;/then they fall down and worship!/They lift it to their shoulders, they carry it,/they set it in its place, and it stands there;/it cannot move from its place./If one cries out to it, it does not answer/or save anyone from trouble.
>
> Remember this and consider,/recall it to mind, you transgressors,/remember the former things of old;/for I am God, and there is no other;/I am God, and there is no one like me (Isa. 46:3-9).

Consider the idols in our own lives that burden us: success, acceptance, our image, security. Our most common expressions of idolatry may stem from unwillingness or inability to accept the fact that in Jesus Christ we see God and we know God's character: Though God is transcendent, in Jesus Christ through the Holy Spirit, God is *near*. If we serve a sovereign God who willingly wraps himself with a towel and washes his disciples' feet, who goes to a cross to suffer and die, how can we make gods of ourselves or turn to idols that are powerless to promise everlasting life?

The heart of the gospel is that God made us in God's image. When we make up our own images, we denigrate our understanding of ourselves as creatures in God's image. We reduce God to our own terms, denying God and the relationship that God longs for with each of us.

Reflecting and Recording

Recall the story of the young man who was making an idol of his business deal and Stuart Briscoe's confession. When have you allowed something to dominate your thinking, time, and attention to the point of becoming (or almost becoming) an idol? Record that experience here.

How do you respond to the Greta Van Susteren story? Was Robin Gerber too tough on her? Would you feel differently if a man rather than a woman were making this commentary? What tempts you to make appearance an idol? Why do women have to break through a glass ceiling for leadership when "the sky is the ceiling" for men? What idolatry does this phenomenon illustrate?

Spend the balance of your time thinking about the image of carrying your idols. List things or commitments that may burden you, and ask yourself: Have I made this an idol?

DURING THE DAY

Register the occasions today when you are guilty of idolatry that places you rather than God in control.

DAY 4
A Jealous God

> [Moses said,] The LORD was angry with me because of you, and he vowed that I should not cross the Jordan and that I should not enter the good land that the LORD your God is giving for your possession. For I am going to die in this land without crossing over the Jordan, but you are going to cross over to take possession of that good land. So be careful not to forget the covenant that the LORD your God made with you, and not to make for yourselves an idol in the form of anything that the LORD your God has forbidden you. For the LORD your God is a devouring fire, a jealous God.—Deuteronomy 4:21-24

One of the sad stories in scripture is that of Moses not being able to cross the Jordan and enter the Promised Land. Moses perceives that the Lord is angry with him because of the people's rebellion. Watching the people go into the Promised Land while he does not is the price of leadership. The leader often bears the burden, the pain, certainly the failure of the people. A sadness prevails: "I am going to die in this land without crossing over the Jordan" (Deut.4:22). But the prophetic voice and visionary leadership also continue in the passage. In his commentary on this passage from Deuteronomy, Walter Brueggemann says:

> The jealous God is a God who will tolerate no disobedience and who will severely punish disobedient Israel (vv. 24-26). . . . The disobedience of Israel leads to land loss in a harsh manner that abrasively subverts Israel's true character. The simple calculus of disobedience/displacement,

by appeal to the jealous God, constitutes the spine of Deuteronomic theology (Brueggemann, *Deuteronomy*, 56).

The thrust of the second commandment is that God is a jealous God. The Hebrew word translated "jealousy" comes from a root word that means "to be red in the face." It "denotes intense emotional reaction to any affront to God's sovereignty and glory. Moreover, the emotion stressed here is overbearing and white hot" (Hauerwas and Willimon, *The Truth About God*, 30). So in the Old Testament, this word *jealousy* does not connect with the human emotion we associate with envy, pettiness, and suspicion. Rather it means that God cares about us and therefore is not indifferent to what we do and how we live. *Jealousy* in this sense is as much a part of the nature of God as are God's love and forgiveness. God is passionately identified and involved with us.

> *There is a connection, a solidarity, a unity of the human race.*

The commandment against idolatry in Exodus 20 closes with an awful word about the consequences of sin for future generations: "punishing the children for the sin of the fathers to the third and fourth generation" (v. 5, NIV). How harsh! Can it be so? What does it mean? It does not mean that innocent unborn generations are going to be punished for the sins of their fathers. The doctrine of individual responsibility is stated over and over again in the Old and the New Testaments. It does mean, however, that present and future generations suffer the consequences of their parents' actions.

Stanley Hauerwas and Will Willimon, professors at Duke University, recount hearing Millard Fuller tell the story of Habitat for Humanity's birth at a gathering on campus. Later that week several people asked them, "How old were Fuller's children when he and his wife pulled up and moved to Americus?" "Behind the question was the modern sentimentality: It's fine for you to have some religious experience if you want, but it's not fine for you to drag your children into it with you, to ask them to sacrifice for your values" (*The Truth About God*, 38). So Hauerwas and Willimon concluded, "The . . . commandment reveals to us the sobering truth that all of us sacrifice our children to some god or another, that all of us parents routinely ask our children to suffer because of our values, and well we should. Our idolatry is, as the first commandment says, passed on as punishment to our children" (*The Truth About God*, 38).

There is a connection, a solidarity, a unity of the human race. War works its ravaging havoc, not only upon those who participate in it but upon those who come after them. Drunkenness and drugs affect not only the ones who are immediate victims but their families and even people beyond their families. Immoral behavior doesn't end with itself but spreads out to invade the lives of those within its circle. Not only does such behavior invade; it sometimes destroys or—if it does not destroy—it maims, brings sorrow and sadness, or causes endless pain.

God does not seek to influence us to be obedient by punishing us. Sin itself is punishment; it is a fact of any life lived without God.

REFLECTING AND RECORDING

Reflect on your feeling and thoughts when you hear the claim: "The Lord is a jealous God."

———— ᴔᴙᴓ ————

Is there anything in your life—any relationship, activity, attitude, feeling about possessions—that would cause God to be jealous? Make some notes.

Rehearse the story of Millard Fuller. Reflect on whether you or someone you know has thought some parents did not have the right to require sacrifice on the part of their children in order to live according to the parents' values.

———— ᴔᴙᴓ ————

Recall and make notes of a memorable situation in which the sin of parents caused "punishment" (suffering) for their children.

What in your life might adversely affect the lives of friends or loved ones?

———— ᴔᴙᴓ ————

Write a brief prayer of praise and confession addressing God as "Loving Father, jealous God."

DURING THE DAY

Seek to engage at least one person in a discussion about the fact that our Lord "is a jealous God" and/or what it means for the sin of parents to bring punishment to children.

DAY 5
What's in a Name?

You shall not make wrongful use of the name of the LORD your God, for the LORD will not acquit anyone who misuses his name.—Exodus 20:7

God's activity beginning at Creation and continuing through redemption is a naming activity. In addition to their poetic beauty, the first chapters of Genesis reveal profound insight. In the process of creation, the natural order alone is not enough; *persons for relationship* are essential for God. So beings are created after God's own image, and persons are named—Adam and Eve, male and female. In the Creation story in Genesis 2, God gives humanity power to name the animals and thus gives us dominion over creation (Gen. 2:19-20).

The *covenant* was a naming event. Hosea captured it when he recorded God's saying, "I will have mercy upon her that had not obtained mercy; and I will say to them which were not my people, Thou art my people; and they shall say, Thou art my God" (2:23, KJV). Israel is called into being, a nation named as God's people.

The coming of Jesus is the ultimate in God's naming activity. The mysterious "I Am" now has a name. Do you remember that "face-to-back" (not face-to-face) encounter of Moses and God? God's self-introduction from the burning bush is, "I am the God of your father, the God of Abraham, the God of Isaac, and the God of Jacob" (Exod. 3:6). Obviously Moses can't grasp that—a God who names God's self as the God of human beings, claiming identity in relationship with persons. Remembering that he is not to look upon God because to do so would mean death, Moses casts the question sidewise over his shoulder: "Who will I tell them you are?" And the answer comes, "I AM WHO I AM" (Exod. 3:13-14).

What kind of answer is that? What a mystery to grapple with! But now we know. The "I Am" is named—flesh, bone, blood. The Word is incarnate, and we know the "I AM" is Jesus. It was not enough for God to name God's self as the God of Abraham, Isaac, and Jacob. God had to become an Abraham, Isaac, or Jacob. So God did, and the name is Jesus.

The naming goes on. The church is born—the new Israel—out of the New Covenant. Peter picks up on this naming activity of God as he recalls Old Testament names to designate the New Testament church: "a chosen race, a royal priesthood, a holy nation" (1 Pet. 2:9). Then Peter takes his cue from Hosea, paraphrasing him: "Once you were not a people,/but now you are God's people;/once you had not received mercy,/but now you have received mercy" (1 Pet. 2:10). We Christians, the church, are named by God as God's people. So this is the work of God in history: naming.

In Bible times, a person's name typically reflected something of his or her character or personality. Naturally then God would care deeply about God's own name. So we have the third commandment: "You shall not take the name of the LORD your God in vain" (NKJV).

This third commandment warns against the sin of trying to take advantage of God. Notice that nothing in the Ten Commandments directly condemns intellectual atheism. Jesus' sharpest and most stinging rebukes were leveled at those who professed to believe but did little or nothing about it and those who tried to use God.

Think of the ways in which we have taken God's name upon ourselves. We who have been baptized into the Christian faith have taken God's name. If we have membership in a church, we have taken God's name. If we have professed our faith in Jesus Christ as Lord and Savior, we have taken God's name. If, as parents, we have had our children baptized, we have taken God's name, for we have pledged ourselves to bring up these children in the knowledge and the love and the fear of God. Those of us who have been married in a Christian ceremony took God's name for we have pledged that our relationship in marriage is for better or for worse, not to be broken by caprice or when difficulty may arise. When we come to the sacrament of the Lord's Supper, we take God's name.

Elton Trueblood was right when he said this commandment is a warning against taking God lightly. We break this commandment when we say we believe in God and accept the ideals of God's kingdom but don't live in ways that show we take God seriously. Living that way is a form of atheism. We may be atheists in practice even though we are Christian in profession. We are atheists when we live much of our lives as though God does not matter.

REFLECTING AND RECORDING

To test the truth that we can be atheists in practice though Christian in profession, spend time reflecting on the following three questions:

What do I think about most when I'm not thinking about my work?

—————— ✸ ——————

How do I spend my leisure time, time not required for my job or keeping the household going?

—————— ✸ ——————

How do I spend my money? Get beyond your normal complaints about the grocery bills, high utility bills, huge house payments, and doctor bills. Look at these realities but look further at how you spend the rest of your money.

—————— ✸ ——————

Put a check (✔) in front of the following commitments you have made:

_____ I have accepted Christ as my Savior and have been baptized.

_____ I have taken the vows of church membership.

_____ My child or my children were baptized as infants.

_____ I was married in a Christian ceremony.

_____ I receive Holy Communion regularly.

If you checked any of these, you have taken God's name upon yourself. Write a prayer of *confession*, acknowledging your failure in honoring God's name, pledging to live a life worthy of bearing God's name.

DURING THE DAY

During this day, register when you or someone you observe seeks to take advantage of God or takes God lightly. Also seek to be aware of occasions when the fact that you have taken God's name upon yourself is challenged, threatened, or tested.

DAY 6
Taking the Lord's Name in Vain

The thought that usually comes to mind when we hear this third commandment is use of profanity—the use of God's name in a vulgar way. There was a day when profanity was condemned—and many sermons have been preached on this third commandment, associating it with the language we use. Today, however, profanity flavors much ordinary conversation. It punctuates most of modern literature. And, for the most part, it goes unnoticed. That's unfortunate because our speech does reflect, to a marked degree, who we are. This commandment does prohibit vulgar profanity, and its message is echoed in warnings against unclean speech of any kind elsewhere in scripture.

> Let no evil talk come out of your mouths, but only what is useful for building up, as there is need, so that your words may give grace to those who hear (Eph. 4:29).

> Entirely out of place is obscene, silly, and vulgar talk; but instead, let there be thanksgiving (Eph. 5:4).

> But now you must get rid of all such things—anger, wrath, malice, slander, and abusive language from your mouth (Col. 3:8).

More important than dictating appropriate language, however,

> this Commandment emphasizes that those who name Yahweh, the God of Israel, as God, are entrusted with a responsibility for upholding God's reputation in the world. All that God has done for us, from the creation of the world through the miracles to the atoning death and the resurrection of Jesus Christ, is distilled into God's name. In addition, the New Testament regularly treats the name of Jesus as a divine name, adding to the Third Commandment the concept of stewardship of the name and reputation of Jesus Christ. To take the name of the Lord in vain, then, is to take in vain the entire history of God's saving grace and to discredit the Gospel of Jesus Christ (Stone, in *Decision* [March 2000], 32).

The Hebrew word for *in vain* occurs often in the Old Testament. It means "to empty of content, to make irrelevant." Here is an example: "Unless the LORD builds the house,/those who build it labor in vain./Unless the LORD guards the city,/the guard keeps watch in vain./It is in vain that you rise up early/ and go late to rest,/eating the bread of anxious toil;/for he gives sleep to his beloved" (Ps. 127:1-2). Three times in these two verses the word *vain* is used. It emphasizes the uselessness of our activity apart from the intervention and blessing of God.

For our labor not to be useless, in vain, we must embrace the presence of Christ and allow the Holy Spirit to permeate every fiber of our being. Change comes not because we have designed it or wanted it but because God, in infinite grace and unfettered mercy, in God's own time and design, brings new life to a person, a congregation, a community. "Unless the LORD builds the house, those who build it labor in vain" (Ps. 127:1). Lawson Stone also reminds us that from this sense of uselessness, indicated by the term "in vain," of ordinary human activity apart from the blessing of God, comes a second meaning of the Hebrew term "in vain": ultimately false and disappointing. That which cannot work effectively will ultimately be proved false.

> Substituting the sense of ineffectiveness, fruitlessness, uselessness, and deceitfulness for the traditional "in vain" of the Commandment produces a shocking result. The declaration in the Third Commandment that we are not to take the reputation and saving work of our covenant—keeping God "in vain" points far beyond saying a form of God's name in an angry tone. What it tells us is not to let God's name, and all that it implies, be ineffectual and meaningless in our lives" (Stone, in *Decision* [March 2000], 32).

Our stance, then, is on our knees praying, "Lord, have mercy on me, a sinner; renew me, quicken me, empower me." But also standing erect, affirming: "The battle is yours, Lord—and the victory is yours. I am your servant. Here am I, send me."

REFLECTING AND RECORDING

Spend a few minutes considering Lawson Stone's challenging assertion that those who claim God's name and "own" God as Lord, "are entrusted with a responsibility for upholding God's reputation in the world."

One meaning of taking the Lord's name in vain is to connect God's name with acts and attitudes devoid of a sincere relationship and dependence on God. Test yourself:

- In what ways do you pray as though you were totally dependent upon the Lord? In what ways do you pray as though dependent but live as though your human resources are all you have?

- In what ways does your worship reflect a sincere awareness of God's active presence in your life, apart from which life would be "useless," without meaning?

- In what ways do your walk and your talk reflect your awareness that all is "useless" and will be "proved false" apart from the intervention and blessing of God?

DURING THE DAY

Register the occasions today when you labor "in vain," or when by your actions or failure to act, by your speech and relationships, you fail to uphold God's reputation in the world.

DAY 7
Reverencing God's Name

> Blessed be the name of the LORD/from this time on and forevermore./From the rising of the sun to its setting/the name of the LORD is to be praised./The LORD is high above all nations,/and his glory above the heavens.—Psalm 113:2-4

*I*f we use the name of God, we must use it in a way true to its meaning and intention. Any use of the name that denies the character of God breaks this commandment. Isaiah warns:

> Hear this, O house of Jacob,/who are called by the name of Israel,/and who came forth from the loins of Judah;/who swear by the name of the LORD,/and invoke the God of Israel,/but not in truth or right (Isa. 48:1).

This may be the supreme form of breaking the commandment—swearing by the name of the Lord but not in truth; mentioning the God of Israel but not in righteousness. Isaiah was warning these people about using the name of God without obeying the revelation they had received from God. They were violating the third commandment. The Gospel of Mark also warns us by citing Isaiah: "In vain do they worship me, teaching human precepts as doctrines" (Mark 7:7).

Certainly to know and to use God's name are at the heart of our worship and our daily living. Prayer requires this dynamic for we pray "in Jesus' name." When we gather in Jesus' name, God promises to be there. When we pray in God's name, God promises to hear and answer. As we affirmed on Day 5 of this week, God named God's self in God's merciful relationship with Israel, and the "I AM" became flesh in Jesus. Knowing God's name and having been named by God, we pray in Jesus' name. Such prayer requires commitment and obligation. It is also our witness of dependency.

The Lord's Prayer offers us guidance for this kind of naming/living, and we see what it means to reverence the name of God rather than profane it. Some biblical scholars believe an incorrect punctuation occurs in some renderings of this prayer: A period follows "hallowed be thy name"; another period follows "thy kingdom come"; then comes "thy will be done, as in heaven, so on earth." There are three petitions in the prayer, and some scholars believe these should be linked together like a triptych, thus changing the punctuation and the meaning. It would read as follows:

> Our Father which art in heaven,
> > Thy name be hallowed,
> > Thy Kingdom come,
> > Thy will be done,
> As in heaven, so on earth.

In this rendering, "As in heaven, so on earth" refers not only to "thy will be done" but also to "thy Kingdom come" and "hallowed be thy name." The hallowing of God's name, the coming of the kingdom, the doing of God's will are different phases of the same thing. We hallow the name of God by submission to God's kingdom and by doing God's will. Underscore that: We submit to God's kingdom and do God's will in order that God's name will be hallowed, not that we might be recognized or honored.

In his short story "Father Sergius," Leo Tolstoy illustrates the most blinding form of vanity—religious vanity. We are guilty of religious vanity when we worship or pray perfunctorily, not intending to match our deeds with our words.

> "I lived for men on the pretext of living for God. . . . But after all was there not some share of sincere desire to serve God?" [the priest] asked himself, and the answer was: "Yes, there was, but it was all soiled and overgrown by desire for human praise. Yes, there is no God for the [person] who lives as I did, for human praise."

That indictment fits too many of us. Even in our serving, we take God's name in vain by becoming ensnared in religious vanity—doing what we do to be recognized and receive the praise of others.

REFLECTING AND RECORDING

Name the three most religious persons you know:

_____   _____   _____

Look at each of these persons in turn. What do they do in service of God? How are they faithful in worship? Note any hint that they do what they do in order to be recognized or praised. In what ways do they exemplify real joy in their religious lives? What kind of credit do they receive in their communities?

Spend a few minutes reflecting on Father Sergius's claim: "There is no God for the [person] who lives . . . for human praise."

———❧———

Spend whatever time you have left reviewing the content of this week. What new insights have come? What questions have been raised? What has been your biggest challenge? Note anything you want to discuss with your group.

DURING THE DAY

Designate three times when you anticipate being alone today.

_____   _____   _____

At those times repeat aloud or think of as many of the commandments as you have memorized.

Group Meeting for Week Three

Leader: You will need a chalkboard or newsprint for this session.

INTRODUCTION

Two essential ingredients for a Christian fellowship are feedback and follow-up. Feedback keeps the group dynamic working positively for all participants. Follow-up expresses Christian concern and ministry.

As leader, you are the one primarily responsible for feedback in the group, but encourage all members to share their feelings about how the group is functioning. Listening is crucial. Listening to one another, as much as any other action, is a means of affirming others. When you listen to another, you are saying, "You are important; I value you." Being sure you understand the meaning of what others say is critical too. We often mishear. "Are you saying _____?" is a good question to check what you've heard. If a couple of persons in a group listen and give feedback in this fashion, they can set the mood for the whole group.

Follow-up is a function for everyone. If we listen to what others are saying, we will discover needs and concerns beneath the surface, situations that deserve special prayer and attention. Make notes of these as the group shares. Follow up during the week with a telephone call, a written note of caring and encouragement, maybe a visit. What distinguishes Christian fellowship is caring in action. Ideally our caring should be so evident that others notice and remark, "My, how those Christians love one another!"

SHARING TOGETHER

By this time you are getting to know one another well; persons are beginning to feel safe in the group and perhaps more willing to share. Still there is no place for pressure. The leader, however, can be especially sensitive to those slow to share. Seek to coax them out gently. Every person is a gift to the group. The gift is fully revealed by sharing.

1. Begin your time together by singing a chorus or stanza from a hymn everyone knows, such as "Amazing Grace."

2. Spend eight to ten minutes letting each participant talk about "how I'm doing" with this workbook. What is positive? negative? Name special meanings, joys, difficulties. Encourage one another.

3. Spend a few minutes talking about this assertion: Whenever anyone or anything usurps the place God should have in our lives, we are guilty of idolatry.

4. Invite a couple of people to share an experience or an ongoing life reality when they allowed something to so dominate their time, energy, and attention that it became—or almost became—an idol.

5. Invite one person to refer back to his or her Reflecting and Recording on the Greta Van Susteren story (Day 3) and share in response to the questions there.

6. Allow group members to spend a few minutes sharing their response when they hear this claim: "The Lord is a jealous God."

7. Ask a couple of persons to share a memorable situation in which the sin of parents caused "punishment" (suffering) for their children.

8. Spend six to ten minutes talking about the possibility of being atheistic in practice though Christian in profession (Day 5).

9. Invite two or three persons to respond to Lawson Stone's challenging assertion that those who claim God's name and "own" God as Lord "are entrusted with a responsibility for upholding God's reputation in the world."

PRAYING TOGETHER

John Wesley gave us a new perspective on Jesus' call to ask, seek, and knock:

> O how meek and gentle, how lowly in heart, how full of love both to God and man, might ye have been at this day, if you had only asked;—if you had continued instant in prayer! Therefore, now, at least, "ask, and it shall be given unto you." Ask, that ye may thoroughly experience, and perfectly practise, the whole of that religion which our Lord has here so beautifully described. It shall then be given you, to be holy as he is holy, both in heart and in all manner of conversation. Seek, in the way he hath ordained, in searching the Scriptures, in hearing his word, in meditating thereon, in fasting, in partaking of the Supper of the Lord, and surely ye shall find: Ye shall find that pearl of great price, that faith which overcometh the world, that peace which the world cannot give, that love which is the earnest of your inheritance. Knock; continue in prayer, and in every other way of the Lord: Be not weary or faint in your mind: Press on to the mark: Take no denial: Let him not go until he bless you. And the door of mercy, of holiness, of heaven, shall be opened unto you (Wesley, *The Works of John Wesley*, vol. 5:401).

Leader: Read aloud the above excerpt as you begin your prayer time.

1. Invite the group to share special prayer concerns. After each concern, ask a volunteer to offer a brief prayer.

2. Invite each member of the group to spend two minutes in quiet prayer for the person whose picture he or she selected in Week 2's group meeting.

3. Close this time of prayer by asking someone to read his or her prayer from Day 4, beginning, "Loving Father, jealous God. . . ."

Week Four

Keeping the Sabbath

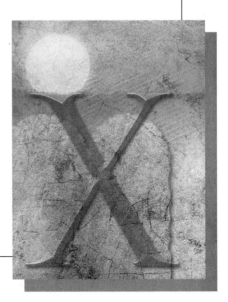

DAY 1
A Matter of Identity

I grew up in a card-playing family who enjoyed games such as canasta, Rook, hearts, and kaloochi. Interestingly, I also grew up in a rigid religious culture. Though my family did not fit into that culture very well, we were significantly affected by it. Playing cards was considered a sin.

I recall being in my parents' home one Sunday afternoon. I had long since finished my theological training, had been ordained as a Methodist preacher, and was serving as a pastor in a growing congregation. I was visiting with my parents, and we had gone to worship at their little Baptist church that morning and had had a wonderful Sunday dinner. After dinner we had removed the dishes from the table and brought out the cards. We were having a happy time when my mother looked out the window and saw her Baptist pastor driving up.

When my mother became excited or was about to say something very important, she would preface it with these words: "Oh Lord God, I do pray." That's the way she began. "Oh Lord God, I do pray—hide the cards, son, here comes the preacher." Her pastor was making a Sunday afternoon call to visit with me as well as them, and my mother didn't want him to "catch us" playing cards—especially on Sunday. Never mind that I too was a preacher. Never mind that I was enjoying myself in a wonderful way, relaxing with my parents, having a good time, playing what we enjoyed most to play—Rook. I doubt if there is a commandment that has been more misunderstood than this one:

> Remember the sabbath day, and keep it holy. Six days you shall labor and do all your work. But the seventh day is a sabbath to the LORD your God; you shall not do any work—you, your son or your daughter, your male or female slave, your livestock, or the alien resident in your towns. For in six days the LORD made heaven and earth, the sea, and all that is in them, but rested the seventh day; therefore the LORD blessed the sabbath day and consecrated it (Exod. 20:8-11).

I also doubt whether we need to understand and heed any commandment more than this one.

As we begin to explore this fourth commandment, recall our discussion during Week 1 regarding reasons for keeping the commandments in the first place. When we strive to keep the commandments, our behavior provides evidence of our love for God and response to God's love for us. Our desire to be obedient is our connection to God; it reflects in an outward and visible way our inward and spiritual relationship with God. That divine-human connection is at the heart of the fourth commandment. In Exodus 31:12, God says, "The sabbath is a sign of the covenant between me and you forever" (AP). And again in verse 17, "It is a permanent sign of my covenant with them" (AP). We need not only relationship but also visible connection as we live out our relationship with God.

The sabbath concerns our identity. Observance of sabbath identified Israel as Israel. No one who knows anything about Israel's history or has any acquaintance with Judaism—especially conservative and orthodox Judaism in our day—would doubt the importance of the sabbath for a Jew. Historically, keeping the sabbath was an inescapable obligation for the Jewish family, and an integral part of their home life. To appreciate the significance of it, call to mind the fact that most Hebrews have lived outside the confines of the Holy Land over the centuries. They lived in "unholy cities" of the Asian or Mediterranean world. They did their work, traded, and lived with Gentiles, who had little or no knowledge of their law—and certainly little understanding or sympathy for their way of life.

When Jews were living in isolated communities in the ancient world, the sabbath was not simply a habit; it was a badge of identity, setting them apart—even setting them over against the culture and habits of the nation and the city in which they lived. Imagine how embarrassing it must have been for them to exercise their identity. They could covet, commit adultery, steal, even worship other gods in secret, but not to observe the sabbath was a public declaration, which carried with it a separation from their people, the people of God.

So, to "remember" the sabbath is more than to recall an idea; it is to bow down and worship. Keeping the sabbath was the distinguishing characteristic of Jews; it was this practice that, more than any other, set them apart and kept them together as Jews. Sabbath is about identity, acknowledging who we are.

REFLECTING AND RECORDING

Make some notes about how your family observed the sabbath during your growing-up years.

Can you recall an experience when you got in trouble for doing something on Sunday that would not have landed you in trouble on another day? Or revisit a conflict between your family's observance of Sunday and the community in which you lived. Make some notes.

List Sunday practices/observances of your growing-up years that you no longer continue.

Reflect on the difference between sabbath observance as a matter of identity for Jews and the way you observe Sunday as a part of your identity. Make notes.

DURING THE DAY

Talk with two or three people this week about the difference between their observance of Sunday during their growing-up years and their observance of Sunday now.

DAY 2
The Sabbath and Sunday

*T*o pursue the notion of identity, which we considered yesterday, we need to remember that the Christian observance of Sunday as "the Lord's Day" grew out of the Jewish practice of sabbath. The commandment related to the sabbath is stated more elaborately than any other in both the Exodus account (20:8-11) and in Deuteronomy:

> Observe the sabbath day and keep it holy, as the LORD your God commanded you. Six days you shall labor and do all your work. But the seventh day is a sabbath to the LORD your God; you shall not do any work—you, or your son or your daughter, or your male or female slave, or your ox or your donkey, or any of your livestock, or the resident alien in your towns, so that your male and female slave may rest as well as you. Remember that you were a slave in the land of Egypt, and the LORD your God brought you out from there with a mighty hand and an outstretched arm; therefore the LORD your God commanded you to keep the sabbath day (Deut. 5:12-15).

There are also other shorter forms recorded, including Exodus 23:12; 34:21; and Leviticus 19:3, where religious laws and rules of conduct are enumerated.

The cultural inclination to cease from work on the seventh day was already in place when Moses met Yahweh on Mount Sinai. The people of that time already observed a seven-day cycle. The sabbath, or seventh day, was accepted as a day when physical labor was discouraged. Even before they received the Ten Commandments, Moses told the Israelites that they needed to learn to rest on the seventh day. When they were wandering through the desert before arriving at Mount Sinai, they relied upon Yahweh to provide them the food needed to stay alive. Yahweh gave them food in the form of manna, which they gathered each day from the ground for the following day. Moses was teaching them to be dependent upon the Lord. They were not to gather more food than they needed for present sustenance. Those who didn't trust in the daily provision of manna and who hoarded it, found their extra supply becoming wormy and rotten (Exod. 16:20).

On the sixth day the people were to gather a double portion because on the seventh day God would provide no manna. God was said to be resting in observance of the sabbath (Exod. 20:11). Those who failed to do what Moses commanded them went out searching for food on the seventh day but found none. God did not distribute it on that day. Those who were obedient to Moses found that their extra ration of manna did not spoil as it did on other days. Even then, before the giving of the Ten Commandments at Mount Sinai, the people learned their lesson, for after that "the people rested on the seventh day" (Exod. 16:30).

The word *sabbath* comes from the Hebrew word that means "to cease or rest." According to scripture, the first motivation given for observing this commandment was the fact that God had first rested on the seventh day. In the Genesis account of creation, after six long days of working at the creation task, God is depicted as sitting down, wiping his brow, and resting. It seemed only right that those who were followers of God would live by God's example. Since nothing was before God's creation, it follows that when God stopped working, God created something that was not there before: leisure, relaxation, rest. So the notion of rest, relaxation, leisure was a planned and essential element of God's creation.

In the Deuteronomic account of this commandment for sabbath observance, the reason given was to have a day of remembering God (Deut. 5:15). God's most gracious act of love for the Israelites was freeing them from slavery in Egypt. But after wandering many years in the desert, the Hebrews lost their sense of Yahweh's wonderful love. They became concerned for bread and water and worried how they were going to reach the Promised Land. Their preoccupation with immediate concerns obscured the original marvelous saving act of Yahweh. God gave them the sabbath command to keep the memory of that original saving event ever present in their community.

By the time of Jesus, sabbath observance . . . had been severely distorted.

The sabbath was to be a day "holy to the LORD" (Exod. 31:15), a day God had already made holy (Exod. 20:11). From sundown of the sixth day to sundown of the seventh day, faithful people were provided a unique opportunity to relate to their God. Through the years, the Hebrews devised all sorts of rules and regulations to support the special nature of the sabbath. At the heart of those was attending the synagogue service at which prayers and psalms were said, a section of the Law and the Prophets read, a homily preached, and a blessing given. The sabbath was also supported by regulations enforcing the prohibition against work. By the time of Jesus, the rabbis had enumerated thirty-nine types of work prohibited on the sabbath. For example, no fires were to be lit, no clapping of hands, no jumping, no slapping the thigh. Even visits to the sick were not allowed because one could walk only about half a mile.

By the time of Jesus, sabbath observance and the meaning of sabbath had been severely distorted. All four Gospels record that Jesus faithfully observed the sabbath by attending the synagogue services and even preaching at them (Matt. 4:23; 9:35; Mark 1:39; Luke 4:15; John 18:20). But Jesus was aware that his mission and his authority were to inject a new spirit into the Jewish religious practices: "the Son of Man is lord even of the sabbath" (Mark 2:28). Though Jesus came, in his own words, "to fulfill the law" (Matt. 5:17), he came to clarify the meaning that God had intended for the laws and the teachings. Thus he lifted the sabbath from the turbulent, tangled trappings that had accumulated through human meddling with God's laws through the centuries and encouraged people to celebrate it with joy and meaning.

REFLECTING AND RECORDING

Yesterday you reflected on how the sabbath was observed during your growing-up years. Continue that reflection, not only on your family's practices but on those of others in your community. Make a list of practices that became attached to the sabbath that had little or nothing to do with God's intention for this commandment.

Yesterday you listed sabbath practices of your growing-up years which are no longer a part of your life. Consider why you have left these practices out of your life.

If the meaning of the Hebrew word for sabbath is "to cease and to rest," how are you incorporating that meaning into the way you keep the sabbath?

DURING THE DAY

Make plans to incorporate an activity or action or to remove an activity or action from your sabbath routine in order to move closer to God's intentions for this commandment.

DAY 3
Rest and Remembering

As we indicated yesterday, teachers of the law had added so many restrictions to the observance of the sabbath, the people could no longer celebrate it with joy and meaning. The many regulations and required religious practices deadened the spirit and obscured the spiritual values present in the law. Jesus sought to restore the sabbath to its original purposes: rest and remembering God's goodness. On at least six distinct occasions, Jesus was engaged in disputes about the sabbath with Jewish leaders. It was his attitude toward the sabbath that first aroused their suspicions and inspired their fierce opposition.

> Again he entered the synagogue, and a man was there who had a withered hand. They watched him to see whether he would cure him on the sabbath, so that they might accuse him. And he said to the man who had the withered hand, "Come forward." Then he said to them, "Is it lawful to do good or to do harm on the sabbath, to save life or to kill?" But they were silent. He looked around at them with anger; he was grieved at their hardness of heart and said to the man, "Stretch out your hand." He stretched it out, and his hand was restored (Mark 3:1-5).

Jesus used the sabbath for humanity, as God intends it. On one sabbath day, he cured a woman who was crippled and drained of strength (Luke 13:10-13). On another sabbath, he cured a man who had been sick for thirty-eight years, saying, "My father's at work until now, and I'm at work as well" (John 5:17, AP). When Jesus cured people on the sabbath, he taught that he was not breaking the sabbath but was true to the intent of the sabbath, not only resting but also remembering the generous care of God for persons. Unless justified by a life-and-death situation, curing people was considered work and thus forbidden. But when Jesus was about to cure a man with a withered hand on the sabbath, he asked the leaders, "Is it lawful to cure on the sabbath?" He knew what their objection would be, so he had a ready answer:

> He said to them, "Suppose one of you has only one sheep and it falls into a pit on the sabbath; will you not lay hold of it and lift it out? How much more valuable is a human being than a sheep! So it is lawful to do good on the sabbath" (Matt. 12:11-12).

Though God "rested" on the sabbath, God continued "work" by keeping all of creation in existence and by watching over people. Jesus remembered this and reminded those around him that as God was his Father, he would "work" lovingly as his Father worked on the sabbath—watching over his people. Jesus' teaching reminds us that keeping the sabbath is not about rigid rules but about perspective, about love, and about God's life-giving power.

The presentation of the Ten Commandments in the Exodus and the Deuteronomy accounts begins, "I am the LORD your God, who brought you out of the land of Egypt, out of the house of slavery" (Exod. 20:2; Deut. 5:6). This word, in which God identifies God's self as the one who delivered Israel from slavery, is repeated as part of the fourth commandment in Deuteronomy. "Remember that you were a slave in the land of Egypt, and the LORD your God brought you out from there with a mighty hand and an outstretched arm; therefore the LORD your God commanded you to keep the sabbath day" (v. 15).

The sabbath was originally designated as a time of remembering. God had delivered Israel out of bondage. The Christian sabbath began with those who experienced Jesus after his resurrection in a new and different way. In the beginning, the Christian Sunday probably had nothing to do with the Jewish sabbath. It was appropriately called "the Lord's Day," and it commemorated our Lord's resurrection from the dead. The early Jewish converts to the Christian faith would have observed their Jewish sabbath as usual. On the following morning they would have gathered for worship, to celebrate the Lord's Supper, and to thank God for the Resurrection.

The centrality of the Resurrection generated a whole new dimension to sabbath celebration for Christians. They chose the first day of the week (Sunday to us) for their sabbath rather than the seventh day, since Jesus rose on the first day of the week (Luke 24:1 ff.). The new spirit given the sabbath prompted these early Christians to change the day's name to "the Lord's Day." In the second century, Saint Ignatius of Antioch said, "Those who were brought up in the ancient order of things have come to the possession of a new hope, no longer observing the Sabbath, but living in the observance of the Lord's Day, on which also our life has sprung up again by Him and by His death" (Ignatius, in *Ante-Nicene Fathers*, vol. 1, 62).

REFLECTING AND RECORDING

Spend a few minutes reflecting on Jesus' insistence that "the sabbath was made for humankind, and not humankind for the sabbath" (Mark 2:27).

———— ❧ ————

How is this claim of Jesus' affecting your observation of sabbath?

———— ❧ ————

One of the original meanings of sabbath was *remembering*. Make some notes about how you practice remembering, not just on one day but in the whole of your life.

In what ways does your reflection on remembering call you to a more intentional observance of sabbath?

———— ❧ ————

DURING THE DAY

Seek four or five occasions during this day to remember the Lord and what the Lord has done for you.

DAY 4
A Right Perspective on Work

> Then the LORD said to me, "Go and stand in the gates of Jerusalem, first at the gate where the king goes out, and then at each of the other gates. Say to all the people, 'Listen to this message from the LORD, you kings of Judah and all you people of Judah and everyone living in Jerusalem. This is what the LORD says: Listen to my warning and live! Stop carrying on your trade at Jerusalem's gates on the Sabbath day. Do not do your work on the Sabbath, but make it a holy day. I gave this command to your ancestors, but they did not listen or obey. They stubbornly refused to pay attention and would not respond to discipline.—Jeremiah 17:19-23, NLT

I'd read the story hundreds of times, but I had missed the impact of one line. It was the Creation story in Genesis and the line was this: "So God blessed the seventh day and hallowed it, because on it God rested from all the work that he had done in creation" (Gen. 2:3).

That line hit me. No other day had God blessed. God didn't bless the day in which God separated the earth from the waters. God didn't bless the day God made the birds of the air and the fish in the sea. God didn't even bless the day God made male and female. Rather God blessed the day of rest. That fact ought to speak to us workaholics, persons who think they don't have time to rest, to play, to worship, simply to "waste time" renewing body, mind, and spirit. On the surface, the commandment to remember the sabbath day and keep it holy does not have the gravity of the others. To remember and rest—not to labor on one day of the week—how serious can this be? It is not easy to accept the fact that if we do not obey the command to rest, we are lawbreakers in God's sight just as much as if we ignore the commandments not to kill, steal, commit adultery, or covet other people's goods.

Yet we keep on asking, how is sabbath relevant to our modern, complicated times? We no longer live in an agrarian culture where the cycles of planting and harvest rule our lives. Our work has changed; our lives have changed. In developed countries, we have become a culture of producers and consumers. Giant industries have replaced small shops. Agriculture has been commercialized. Industrialization and production shape our common life. Work never stops. Lights never go out, day or night. Many of us no longer work Monday through Friday or even nine to five. Stores and restaurants are no longer closed on Sundays, and with the advent of the Internet, some stores are never closed at all. The distinction among days is nearly lost; life marches along regardless of what day it is.

Even animals are included in the specific listing of those who are to do no work on the seventh day. By law, the Tokyo City Zoo, in Japan, must be closed for two days each month. Officials passed this law when they discovered the animals were showing signs of extreme emotional distress from being constantly exposed to the public. If this is true of animals, how much more is it true of humans? We are constantly under pressure, especially as we must relate to lots of other people. We need to take time—time to rest our bodies, to let our minds slow down, to give some ease to our souls, to reflect and pray, to worship, to deepen relationships with those who love us so their love might restore our souls in turn.

The fourth commandment addresses the urge to be always doing. This commandment directly relates to how we feel about our lives and how we feel about God. Not only does it make a demand but it also informs us about the nature of the God who is making this demand.

> For in six days the LORD made the heavens, the earth, the sea, and everything in them; then he rested on the seventh day. That is why the LORD blessed the Sabbath day and set it apart as holy (Exod. 20:11, NLT).

God knows the value of work and the value of rest and keeps them in perspective. When God rested on the seventh day, God gave us a model for the perspective we need to balance work and rest appropriately.

It is God who is at work in the world, not us. We may be busy, but God is the One truly at work. When we fail to rest, we dishonor God, working as though we can accomplish what in reality only God can accomplish through us. Our continual work signifies our own feelings of self-importance. That is a significant point to ponder. What in our lives is so important that we cannot put it aside for a brief period of time?

REFLECTING AND RECORDING

To what degree do you think this commandment is as important as the others?

Make some notes about the nature of your life—work, relationships, community—that prevents you from observing Sunday however you choose.

To what degree do you have to feel busy in order to feel worthwhile?

DURING THE DAY

Observe the activity and work of people around you today. What is their attitude toward their work, their busyness? Do they feel their work won't get done if they don't do it? In what ways do they find their identity and value in their work? How much like them are you?

Keep asking yourself: How can I make my work a sacrament to God?

DAY 5
A Right Perspective on Rest

> Tell the people of Israel to keep my Sabbath day, for the Sabbath is a sign of the covenant between me and you forever. It helps you to remember that I am the LORD, who makes you holy. . . . It is a permanent sign of my covenant with them. For in six days the LORD made heaven and earth, but he rested on the seventh day and was refreshed.—Exodus 31:13, 17, NLT

*I*n her book *Keeping the Sabbath Wholly,* Marva J. Dawn makes the case for *ceasing, resting, embracing,* and *feasting* as ways to keep the sabbath *wholly.* She dedicates the book to all the people who need the sabbath—

> the busiest, who need to work from a cohesive, unfragmented self; . . .
> those who chase after fulfillment and need to understand their deepest yearnings and to hear the silence; . . .
> those who are alone and need emotional nourishment;
> those who live in community and need solitude;
> those who cannot find their life's priorities and need a new perspective; . . .
> those who long for deeper family life and want to nurture certain values; . . .
> those who are disgusted with dry, empty, formalistic worship and want to love and adore God;
> those who want to be God's instruments, enabled and empowered by the Spirit to be world changers and Sabbath healers (Dawn, *Keeping the Sabbath Wholly,* dedication page).

We are all included. We need to *cease* our continual activity. And we need to *rest.* Sabbath keeping, taking one day out of seven, reminds us of the rhythm of life required to be whole persons. God desires us to rest because rest is crucial to our well-being, an integral part of our physical and spiritual health.

Rest restores creative passion to our lives. It reminds us that one of the main characteristics of a Christ-follower is freedom. Many of us have invented a new kind of slavery—a voluntary slavery. We are slaves to our work, whatever that may be, whether it is paid or unpaid.

Real rest refocuses our attention on God, the God who gives us freedom. It reminds us that if it were not for God, our lives would simply move from one enslavement to the next. Perhaps you have observed, as we have, two sorts of people who visit art galleries. There are the mere vagrants who are always on the move, passing from picture to picture without seeing anything. And then there are the students who sit down and contemplate. They meditate and saturate themselves in the beauty and meaning of the art. People's responses to life are the same. Our hectic lifestyle turns too many of us into vagrants, moving from one experience or encounter to another. We never stop to ask, *What does this mean?* or *What was John really saying?* We act similarly in relation to God as well. We don't take time simply to be still and listen—to probe meaning and to ask what God may want to do with our lives. The sabbath can be time we treat as God's time, resting with God, loving and receiving love.

REFLECTING AND RECORDING

Make a list of what provides you *rest*—*not* restricted to a particular day.

What do you do on Sunday, apart from worship, that not only disengages you from work but is a *re-creating* practice? Make notes.

If you could order your Sunday any way you pleased, what would it look like? Make notes.

DURING THE DAY

Begin to think forward to this coming Lord's Day. Incorporate part of what you have just recorded as your desire for Sunday into your plans for next Sunday.

DAY 6
Doing Nothing and Doing Something

The LORD of hosts is with us;/the God of Jacob is our refuge./Come, behold the works of the LORD;/see what desolations he has brought on the earth./He makes wars cease to the end of the earth;/he breaks the bow, and shatters the spear;/he burns the shields with fire./"Be still, and know that I am God!/I am exalted among the nations,/I am exalted in the earth."/The LORD of hosts is with us;/the God of Jacob is our refuge.—Psalm 46:7-11

We continue to ask, "How do we keep the commandment not to work on the sabbath?" One of Jesus' main arguments with the Pharisees was that they had made the sabbath too complicated. The many rules about what was work and what was not made observing sabbath virtually impossible to do with any depth of spirit. So how do we negotiate that terrain?

Sabbath keeping involves two seemingly contradictory elements—doing "nothing" and doing "something." Doing "nothing" is actually the harder of the two because we are not just to do nothing; we are to do *absolutely* nothing.

Back in the 1950s Halford E. Luccock wrote letters to *The Christian Century* under the pen name Simeon Stylites. In one letter he explained how he chose his pseudonym but also wrote an informative word about sabbath keeping. He quoted George Lamb, who said Saint Simeon had a "terrific talent for doing nothing." Luccock went on to explain that is a real art. Many people think they are doing nothing when they are merely doing something trivial, such as fiddling at something, dawdling, playing solitaire, or worrying about the work they should be doing. Thus they miss it on both ends. They do not accomplish anything, and they do not enter the "Beatific State of Pure Vacancy" (Luccock, *Like a Mighty Army*, 79–80).

We do nothing so that our souls can catch up with our bodies.

Not only are we to do nothing; we are also to do nothing for a reason. We do nothing so that our souls can catch up with our bodies, or so that our bodies can just catch up. We do nothing so that in the silence of nothing we can hear ourselves think again—or feel again—or imagine again—or create again. We do nothing so that in the silence of nothing we can hear God thinking again—or feeling again—or imagining again—or creating again through us. We do nothing for the sake of God.

The reason for doing nothing is detachment. We seek to do nothing in order to break loose from the hectic lifestyle that keeps us in bondage to doing and getting, using and spending, consuming and engaging. It is the dynamic of "letting go," seeking to experience, at least for a time, a mind that does not cling to anything.

We know by heart and quote often the first part of Psalm 46:10: "Be still, and know that I am God!" We need to pay attention to the balance of the verse: "I am exalted among the nations, I am exalted in the earth." The Hebrew word translated "be still" may also be translated "cease striving." It means to relax, to let the hand release its grip, to slow down, in fact, to stop. This is not easy. Our minds cling to everything. Not to be concerned, even preoccupied, with what happened yesterday or what may happen tomorrow is almost impossible. But this is the aim of detachment and the reason sabbath is essential. Isn't it true that the more attached we are to possessions, outcomes, security, protective attitudes, even relationships, the less free and happy we are? Whatever has our attention and takes our attention away from God is an idol we put in God's place. Detachment refocuses attention from being centered in self to being centered in God.

While keeping the sabbath may mean doing "nothing," it may also mean doing something. It may mean doing something that we wouldn't be able to do if we did not have sabbath—the activities we would not do if every day was a workday: relaxing with family and friends, playing sports, reading. The nothing of sabbath is what we do for God's sake; the something of sabbath is what we do for our sake and for the sake of our relationships.

REFLECTING AND RECORDING

Spend some time asking yourself the following questions:

When was the last time I spent at least three hours doing absolutely nothing?

———— ≈≈≈ ————

When was the last time I spent at least two hours doing absolutely nothing for a reason?

———— ≈≈≈ ————

When was the last time I had a sabbath experience that resulted in detachment, enabling me to move from being centered in self to being centered in God?

———— ≈≈≈ ————

Make a list of the things you do on your sabbath that you could not do if you did not at least have a possible sabbath day.

Look carefully at the list you have just made. Which of those things serve to unite you more solidly with Christ? Which of them serve to renew you in body and mind? Which serve to enrich your relationship with those you care for?

———— ≈≈≈ ————

Looking at your list again, could any information there lead you to change your sabbath observance—to pay more attention to a particular area of concern?

DURING THE DAY

Continue thinking about your coming sabbath day. Plan for your above reflections to shape that day—and sabbath days ahead.

DAY 7
Exposing Ourselves to God's Company

Verse 11 of Psalm 46 echoes verse 7 of the psalm: "The Lord of hosts is with us; the God of Jacob is our refuge." The repetition underscores the truth that we keep the sabbath holy in order to have a sense of God's presence in all our days. Read again Psalm 46:7-11 on page 77.

Anthony de Mello points out that "faith comes as a gift from just exposing yourself to God's company" (De Mello, *Contact with God*, 58). It will help us in working out our own sabbath observance and our own celebration of "the Lord's Day," to begin at that point. We must find the time to deliberately nourish our souls, to expose ourselves in an intentional way to God's company. In our culture of instant gratification, it's easy to fall into the snare of thinking that somehow the development of the spiritual life is a natural, easy process. We're always tempted to look for shortcuts, to find specific kinds of things that may relieve us of our loneliness and feeling of separation from God. The truth is, there are no shortcuts—and the cultivation of an authentic spirituality requires deliberately exposing ourselves to God's company. One primary way of doing that is keeping a sabbath.

Most of our lives are lived at top speed. In fact, "life on the run" describes most of us. Advertisements entice us to buy cars that are faster and more exciting than the ones we are now driving. How many of us get impatient when the airplane on which we're traveling is delayed for takeoff because of a minor mechanical mishap? What a sight it is in airport terminals to see people, immediately on leaving the airplane, pull out their cell phones and begin conversations even as they walk through the terminal. We laugh at "snail mail" compared to e-mail. We get live television coverage from all over the world. We use palm-size computers to keep up with our "friends" and to do our business. We are addicted to the moment—the immediate—the "urgent."

None of this may be bad—certainly not evil. The question is not whether this fast-paced life is good or efficient but whether it's distracting. These distractions translate into a life lived on the surface—"life on the run." Being able to connect by fax and phone does not enhance our God connection.

While we affirm that all life is "holy," we do not live that reality unless we force ourselves to make it all holy. Keeping sabbath can assist us in remembering that all is holy. Rabbi Menchen Mendal said, "Whoever does not see God in every place does not see God in any place" (Raz, *Hasidic Wisdom,* 19). That radical assertion, if we accept its truth, demands a new way of living on a day-to-day basis.

Sometimes we hear a person say, "I must collect myself" or "I must get myself together." *Recollection* is a core practice called for by spiritual writers of the past. It describes concentrating the attention on the presence of God. It refers to a particular dynamic or stage of prayer in which we still ourselves completely in order to commune with God without hindrance.

More generally, recollection is a dynamic of keeping the sabbath holy. We use one day for primary focus (recollection) in order that our awareness of God will be sensitized, enhanced, informed, and strengthened to hold all our life within this awareness.

It is essential that we not separate our sabbath acts, thoughts, and attitudes from the rest of life. We can easily disconnect participation in worship and religious activities from all else we do. What we seek in sabbath keeping is God's company that does not leave us. God's presence may be experienced in special ways at special times, but that is not the end or goal of authentic Christian spirituality. We remember the sabbath day and keep it holy in order to have a sense of God's presence in all our days.

REFLECTING AND RECORDING

Read the following words of Jesus slowly and deliberately: "Come to me, all you that are weary and are carrying heavy burdens, and I will give you rest. Take my yoke upon you, and learn from me; for I am gentle and humble in heart, and you will find rest for your souls. For my yoke is easy, and my burden is light" (Matt. 11:28-30).

Read the passage again, receiving it as Jesus' personal invitation to you.

———— ❦ ————

When Jesus says, "I will give you rest," his meaning is "I will refresh you." Jesus' rest comes even in the midst of activity, when we give ourselves to him and to others. Ponder this thought: When we take Jesus' yoke upon us, we know rest at the center of our being. We have rest now and the promise of eternal rest.

———— ❦ ————

The sabbath is a time of recognizing need, for receiving the promises of Christ, and for being refreshed by the confidence that his presence can be an ongoing reality. Write a prayer of commitment to ordering your life for sabbath keeping.

DURING THE DAY

Think of a person who needs to hear a word about sabbath keeping. Is there a way you can not only speak that word, but assist that person in actually having a sabbath time?

On page 167 this truth is printed: *God is everywhere, but to find God anywhere, we must meet God somewhere.* Cut this saying out and put it in a place where you can read it many times each day.

Group Meeting for Week Four

INTRODUCTION

Paul advised the Philippians, "Let your conversation be as it becometh the gospel of Christ" (Phil. 1:27, KJV). Life is found in communion with God and also in conversation with others. John Wesley once described the church as a fellowship in which one loving heart sets another heart on fire.

Most of us may not have yet seen the dynamic potential of the kind of conversation to which Paul calls the Philippians. Speaking and listening with the sort of deep meaning that energizes us is not easy. All of us have experiences that are not easy to talk about. Therefore, listening and responding to what we hear is important. Really listening to another person, and reflecting back to him/her what you thought he/she said, helps that person to think clearly and gain perspective. Listening, then, is an act of love. When we listen to someone, we say nonverbally, "I value you. You are important." When we listen in a way that makes a difference, we surrender ourselves to the other person, saying, "I will hear what you have to say and will receive you as I receive your words." When we speak in a way that makes a difference, we speak for the sake of others; thus we are contributing to their understanding and wholeness.

SHARING TOGETHER

1. Ask the group if anyone would like to share anything special connected with using this workbook that has happened during the past week or two.

2. Spend a few minutes talking about how persons are using the During the Day suggestions and what kind of difference their use is making.

3. Spend five to eight minutes sharing how participants' families observed the sabbath during their growing-up years. How is that different from present-day celebrations?

4. What new ideas or understandings of the sabbath did people discover this week? Let each person who is willing share with the group. Take ten to twelve minutes.

5. Invite group members to describe what they would do if they could celebrate Sunday as the sabbath in an ideal way. Take ten to fifteen minutes.

6. Spend four to six minutes discussing each of the following:
   • Sabbath means to cease and desist.
   • How might we practice doing nothing for a reason?
   • What is the role of detachment in sabbath practice?

7. Spend the balance of your time talking about the need for sabbath keeping and sabbath time that is different from "the Lord's Day." How might persons in the group design and order such sabbath time on a regular basis?

PRAYING TOGETHER

Leader: Begin the prayer time by reading Psalm 46 in your Bible and Matthew 11:28-30 printed under Reflecting and Recording on Day 7 of this week. Invite the group to sit in silence for two minutes, allowing these words to create a brief sabbath time.

Sharing prayers of our hearts with others not only confirms our prayerful desires and claims but also inspires the prayers of others. And as Matthew 18:20 promises, Jesus is present for such community prayer. Guide the group in considering the following:

1. Corporate prayer is one of the great blessings of Christian community. Go deeper now, experimenting with the possibilities of corporate prayer by sharing in the fashion described here.

   - Bow in silence and in prayerful concern. The leader calls the name of a person in the group, and someone else in the group offers a brief prayer for the individual named.

   - The leader calls another name and that person is prayed for.

   - The prayers may be brief—two or three sentences—or longer. The leader says to the group, "Think of the person whose name is called. What concern or need has been shared here or in the past weeks that could be mentioned in prayer? You may want to express gratitude for the person's life and witness, the role he or she plays in the group, or that person's ministry in the community. Someone may be seeking direction or may need to make a crucial decision." Let someone pray for each individual in a particular way.

2. Close by singing a familiar chorus or stanza of a hymn.

Week Five

All in the Family

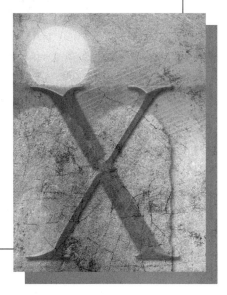

DAY I
Honoring Parents

Honor your father and your mother, so that your days may be long in the land that the LORD your God is giving you.—Exodus 20:12

Honor your father and your mother, as the LORD your God commanded you, so that your days may be long and that it may go well with you in the land that the LORD your God is giving you.—Deuteronomy 5:16

*I*n his article "Kids of the Kingdom," David L. Roper tells of a preacher friend who was visiting a children's Bible class. He asked the children why they loved God. After a few moments a small voice in the back piped up, "I guess it just runs in the family" (www.PreachingToday.com 1/7/02).

This week we will be dealing with two separate but related commandments, both having to do with family: the fifth—honor your father and your mother; and the seventh—do not commit adultery. The fifth commandment shifts our focus from our relationship with God to our relationship with other people. Appropriately, the first commandment regarding relationships with others deals with families, indicating the importance God places on family. The seventh commandment also relates to family relationships, focusing on the most intimate of those relationships, that with a spouse. It indicates the importance God places on faithfulness.

In the arena of earthly relationships, the family is the foundation for everything else. In the family we learn the basic life skills we will need for the rest of our lives—skills such as respecting others and working out conflict. In the family we develop our work ethic. It is where we learn how to live in community. Family is the environment where basic values are taught and become ingrained in our consciences. If we do not learn to live together in the family, learning to get along anywhere else is very difficult.

What does it mean to honor our parents? At the heart of this commandment lies the biblical meaning of honor: to recognize someone's importance. Misunderstanding the word *honor* can cause confusion about this commandment. In English the word *honor* is synonymous with words like *respect* and *admiration*. When we honor, respect, or admire someone, we hold that person in high regard. Holding our parents in high regard is not the call of this commandment. We are commanded to behave toward them in ways that reflect their status as parents. When we honor our parents in this biblical sense, we recognize that our parents' importance and status as parents are objective realities, regardless of whether we think it should be so.

A special connection exists between our parents and God. We honor our parents as the ones who gave us life, just as we honor God, the ultimate Creator and sustainer of all life. The connection continues as honoring our parents teaches us to honor God.

From God's perspective, parents are important for another reason as well. They are responsible for transmitting faith and morality. Parents are crucial links in the chain that leads from humanity to God. God tells Moses to speak to Israel, saying:

> Commit yourselves wholeheartedly to these commands I am giving you today. *Repeat them again and again to your children.* Talk about them when you are at home and when you are away on a journey, when you are lying down and when you are getting up again (Deut. 6:6-7, NLT; emphasis added).

A study has shown that if both parents attend church regularly, 72 percent of their children remain faithful in attendance. If only the father attends regularly, 55 percent remain faithful. If only the mother attends regularly, the percentage drops to 15 percent. If neither attends regularly, only 6 percent of children remain faithful (*Leadership*, vol. 2, no. 3, at www.PreachingToday.com 1/7/02). In an ever-widening circle, the loss of one child to the faith will often lead to an entire family that is lost to the faith. Not too many generations need to pass before an entire community of unbelief has been set in motion.

REFLECTING AND RECORDING

Note the characteristics you admire most about your parents under each heading.

<u>Mother</u>   <u>Father</u>

To honor our parents in the biblical sense, we recognize that our parents' importance and status as parents are objective realities. Consider your relationship with your parents. If you accepted this truth—that parents are to be honored simply because they are parents—how would your attitudes and feelings toward them change?

———————

Spend some time reflecting on the role your parents had in the transmission of faith to you, in the shaping of your moral values.

———————

DURING THE DAY

If either or both of your parents are alive, call them or write them a note thanking them for being your parents and for what they have meant in your life. Even if the only thing you can thank them for is your birth, do so. If your parents are not living, call and affirm someone you know who is doing a good job of parenting.

DAY 2
Honoring—No Matter What

*D*espite understanding the objective nature of biblical honoring, many people find the fifth commandment a seemingly insurmountable hurdle. Apart from the independent importance of parents, family relationships are complex and the interpersonal dynamic between parents and children can be filled with conflict. Some people are fortunate enough to move through adolescence and adulthood with a strong bond of attachment and love for their parents, while for others the relationship barely survives. For others still, too much painful history may prevent reaching adulthood with any love for their parents. Emphasizing what it means to honor can help in negotiating this emotional minefield.

Tension often marks the parent-child relationship. While complex or tragic reasons may underlie tension, at a basic level tension arises simply because children usually believe they know more than their parents and parents usually desire to share life-lessons with their children. These simple yet contradictory forces inevitably lead to conflict. Note that this commandment does not say to love your parents. In fact, nowhere in the Bible are we commanded to *love* our parents. To be sure, the commands to love God, strangers, and neighbors include our parents. But the commandment specifically related to parents says to *honor*. God gave us the commandment to honor our parents as a way of ensuring that, even if the older generation does not feel wanted by their families or by society, those persons still will be given their appropriate reward. God's command balances the tension-filled relationship between parents and children so that even in the absence of love, a thread will keep parents and children attached.

When we confuse loving our parents with honoring them, we set ourselves up for failure. Parents are not perfect. That is why God did not connect the honoring of parents with their merit as parents. Honoring parents who have been responsible and loving can be a simple thing; yet bad parents are to be honored as well, even if we are able to do it at only a nominal level. In some cases, honoring may mean holding our parents accountable. If our parents are abusive, honoring may mean placing distance between us so that they cannot continue to sin against us. It may mean praying for them so that they can see where they have gone wrong. If our parents are unfaithful, honoring may mean that we call for righteousness and, even more importantly, that we are willing to forgive them when they repent.

Ultimately the fifth commandment aims to strengthen the chain linking us with God. Regardless of the challenge, each of us honors our ancestry by being adults who, through our own actions and behavior, add to the greater good of our community and world. In this sense, we honor either what our parents actually live, teach, and represent, or we honor what our parents should live, teach, and represent. In either instance, honor is given.

Society often undermines the call to honor our parents. Rather than asserting that children should honor their parents, the message sent by society is often, "Fathers and Mothers, do your job right." Lives can be damaged when parents do not do their jobs right, but the overall balance God intends for families is skewed when children are placed at the center of family life and parents are assumed to exist to serve children's needs. This perspective places responsibility for problems completely on the shoulders of parents and leaves no room for children to develop a sense of their own personal responsibility.

Movies and television often depict parents as idiots, encourage children to look down on them, and view them as nothing more than a nuisance. But in our dual roles as both child and parent, we are commended by God to refute the perversions of the culture in which we live. When we honor our parents—no matter what—we model for our children the kind of parents they may some day strive to be.

REFLECTING AND RECORDING

Spend a bit of time considering the following questions:

In what ways have you considered *honoring* the same as *loving* in this commandment?

———— ✺ ————

How have you failed to honor one or both parents because you felt they were not worthy?

———— ✺ ————

In relation to your parents, or, if you have children, in their relation to you, how has society undermined the dynamic of honoring mother and father?

———— ✺ ————

What failures or mistakes did your parents make in parenting you that you don't want to make in relation to your children? List them.

In what ways are you allowing these mistakes or failures to affect your relationship with your parents negatively?

———— ✺ ————

Write a prayer expressing to God what you feel about your parents. If confession and repentance are in order, do so.

DURING THE DAY

Think of a person you know who is having difficulty with his or her parent or parents or children. Pray for him or her and find a way to offer support and encouragement.

DAY 3
Children, Obey Your Parents

O n Day 1 of this week, we asserted the objective importance and value of parents—an importance that stands apart from the merits of a particular parent. We discussed the fact that from a biblical perspective, parents are honored not because of their individual ability to parent but because of the objective reality that they gave us *life*. Parents are also important because of their God-given responsibility to transmit faith to their children. Our honoring therefore relates to the value God endows to all parents simply because they are parents.

Joseph A. Califano Jr., president of the National Center on Addiction and Substance Abuse, comments, "Mothers and fathers who are parents rather than pals can greatly reduce the risk of their children smoking, drinking, and using drugs." A center study found that when parents establish rules in their homes, they have better relationships with their teenagers, who have a substantially lower risk of smoking, drinking, and using illegal drugs than the typical teen. Not surprisingly, of the approximately one thousand teens between ages twelve and seventeen involved in the study, only 25 percent live with parents who establish and enforce rules at home. Significantly, these 25 percent are at less risk than teens whose parents do not impose rules (www.PreachingToday.com 1/7/02).

As Califano indicates, we are to be parents, not pals. The goal of the fifth commandment is to instill in children recognition of their parents' inherent authority. From that platform of authority, parents can then fulfill their responsibility to nurture the growth of their children.

But how exactly do we recognize the inherent authority of our parents? While there is much more involved, we want to focus on three things: obedience, respect, and acceptance. Today we will look at obedience. Our role in teaching our children to be obedient is a necessary part of our responsibility as parents to be transmitters of the faith in order to begin their journey toward a life of significance in relationship with God.

As children we honor our parents through obedience. Paul writes to the Ephesians, "Children, obey your parents because you belong to the Lord, for this is the right thing to do. 'Honor your father and mother.' This is the first of the Ten Commandments that ends with a promise. And this is the promise: If you honor your father and mother, 'you will live a long life, full of blessing'" (Eph. 6:1-3, NLT). This does not mean blindly doing whatever our parents tell us; sometimes parents can be wrong. However, generally speaking, parents can capably judge what is in their child's best interest.

When Paul tells the Ephesian children to obey their parents because it is the right thing to do, he includes the key phrase "because you belong to the Lord." The meaningful parallel between God and parents informs the heart of the fifth commandment. Parental authority and the obedience of children are grounded in our relationship with God. Parents are to be to their children what God is to the world. When we live our lives in harmony with God's commandment to honor our parents, we are recognizing that both parents and children are links in a chain that leads directly to God. As parents, our authority over our children is always tempered by God's direction in our lives. As children, obedience is the most basic activity of honoring. As we mature, we obey in keeping with God's will and law, and thus honoring no longer means unquestioned obedience. It is mitigated by accountability to God on both our part and that of our parents. Rather than honoring through simple obedience as we did when we were younger and less mature, we honor by holding our parents and ourselves accountable to God's moral order. We honor our parents by acting in ways that demonstrate our confidence in their capacity for responsible action.

REFLECTING AND RECORDING

Spend a few minutes pondering this statement: Parents are to be to their children what God is to the world.

In what ways were your parents to you as God is to the world? Make some notes.

In what ways are you to your children as God is to the world? Make some notes.

Did your parents' way of teaching and requiring obedience shape you positively or negatively? How might your parents have provided more or less boundaries and discipline?

DURING THE DAY

Observe the people with whom you have contact today, seeking to ascertain how they were shaped by their parents.

DAY 4
Respect and Acceptance

The LORD spoke to Moses, saying: Speak to all the congregation of the people of Israel and say to them: You shall be holy, for I the LORD your God am holy. You shall each revere your mother and father, and you shall keep my sabbaths: I am the LORD your God.—Leviticus 19:1-3

While simple obedience is crucial to honoring our parents when we are younger, as we mature, honoring becomes more complex. As children become more responsible and mature, parents allow them more opportunities to make decisions rather than always requiring obedience to parental decisions. Parents trust not only that the foundations laid during childhood will provide the tools young people need for healthy living but that God will guide them as they choose how to live their lives. Accordingly the call for honoring parents by obedience is transformed to emphasize respect and acceptance.

Kavod is the Hebrew word for "honor." It comes from the word *kavad*, which means "heavy." That is a telling point. Treating our parents with respect may not come naturally to us when their way of living does not merit our respect. While respect involves feelings, at a basic level it can be a simple matter of behavior. In Leviticus 19:3, God commands, "Each of you must show respect for your mother and father" (NLT). The New Revised Standard Version uses the word *revere*. In Jewish tradition the fifth commandment coupled with God's word in Leviticus were two sides of the same coin—a positive and a negative. To honor one's parents was to make sure they were fed, clothed, and had shelter. Thus we demonstrate honor through our acts of kindness and caring.

Honoring means moving beyond those regrets to acceptance.

Reverence, on the other hand, dictated what one refrained from doing: One was not to stand or sit in a parent's reserved place or contradict what a parent said. Thus we demonstrate reverence when we avoid behaving in ways that weaken our parents' authority or that might embarrass them in front of others.

At a bare minimum, this kind of respect demands courteous behavior on our part and responsible care. We make sure that our parents are cared for when they can no longer care for themselves, which may mean we take on that responsibility ourselves or that we make sure it is done by responsible adults, whether in our parents' home or in an appropriate care facility. For some of us, this kind of behavior reflects the deeper love we have for our parents; for others it may be all we are able to muster. In either case, our behavior shows honor of our parents.

Proverbs 1:8-9 says, "Listen, my child, to what your father teaches you. Don't neglect your mother's teaching. What you learn from them will crown you with grace and clothe you with honor" (NLT). Our parents know us better than we may realize. They are also a few steps ahead of us on the journey of life. Honoring them by respecting their counsel and the wisdom they have to offer strengthens the chain that binds us not only to them but, through them, to God.

The final element in honoring our parents is acceptance. All parents are flawed, imperfect human beings, just as each of us is a flawed, imperfect human being. Along with the rest of us, they make mistakes. Being a parent is never an exact science. Even if you read all the books available, you will never have the definitive answer to being a good parent. In fact, reading all the books may be confusing, given how much attitudes toward parenting change over the years from a medical-psychological standpoint as well as a cultural perspective.

Not all parents do a good job—sad but true. But another truth is that most parents earnestly try to do their best. As adults, honoring our parents often means accepting that they did the best they could. Their choices may not have been what we would have wanted and sometimes not what we needed. There may be regrets all around. But honoring means moving beyond those regrets to acceptance.

Acceptance may be the hardest part of honoring because it touches on the very heart of our experience with our parents. Even the best parent-child relationships are fraught with tension and occasional conflict. As children seek independence from their parents and as parents seek to guide and protect their children, conflict is inevitable. Our actions and words can cause pain that lingers long after an event has passed. When parents have been abusive, neglectful, or absent, blame clearly rests on their shoulders, but in most cases, children and parents share responsibility for difficulties in their relationships. Through the process of acceptance, children and parents acknowledge appropriate responsibility and offer appropriate forgiveness to one another.

For some of us with healthy and strong parent-child relationships, the fifth commandment poses no difficulty. But for those whose relationships are filled with pain, just the mention of the commandment to honor our parents opens a Pandora's box. Ignoring these issues does not serve our best interest when we are connected to a community of faith, where burdens are carried together and we share in the work of reconciliation. Relationship with people who can offer us spiritual guidance and support, who can travel with us down the sometimes-difficult road to reconciliation and healing, calls for time beyond Sunday mornings. Time spent in mutual sharing and study with a smaller group of people encourages development of trusting relationships. Be aware, though, that some issues may be too big for a small faith group to handle alone.

Honoring our parents involves recognizing where we have come from and where we are going. It involves recognizing our own responsibility in making family relationships what they are, not only as those relationships develop during childhood years but also as those relationships continue once children have reached adulthood. When we are able to accept our parents as they are, forgiving their imperfections and lifting up their talents and abilities, we will have fulfilled in the deepest sense God's command that we honor our parents.

REFLECTING AND RECORDING

Describe what it means to respect parents.

Think about your relationship with your parents. Describe how you showed respect as you were growing up. How have your attitudes about respect changed? How are you helping your children understand that respecting you is important?

Describe what accepting our parents means.

Think about your relationship with your parents. Describe the role of acceptance in your relationship. How have your attitudes about acceptance changed? How are you teaching and modeling respect in a way that will help your children relate to you?

DURING THE DAY

If you have children, seek the opportunity to talk to them about what you have been feeling and thinking over the past four days about obeying, respecting, and accepting parents as a way of honoring them.

    If talking with children is not possible, find someone to have a conversation with on this important subject.

DAY 5
Living an Honorable Life

*I*n *Christian Reader* (vol. 35, no. 2), Stephen E. Freed writes about watching his father slowly deteriorate from an incurable disease. The painful process had raised many difficult questions in his mind. At one point he asked his fifteen-year-old daughter, Elizabeth, "What will you do if I end up like Granddaddy someday?" As if all the questions his father's illness had raised weren't difficult enough, her response gave Freed even more to think about. "I don't know, Dad," she answered after a moment. "But I'm watching you to find out" (www.PreachingToday.com 1/7/02).

Our children watch us. Parents need to teach children what it means to honor parents and to show them what an honorable life looks like. This requires time. Studies of teenagers show that 66 percent spend less than thirty minutes a week talking with their fathers about things that really matter to them (www.PreachingToday.com 1/7/02). If our children are going to see what an honorable life looks like, we must at a minimum give them our deliberate attention and time. Honor must be modeled, and if we do not spend time with our children, the opportunity to provide that modeling won't materialize.

Throughout the Bible, God's blessing is a sign of God's love. Likewise, human blessing is a sign of love given by one person to another, a deliberate passing on of our love. Blessing does not occur haphazardly, without thought; rather, it is purposeful and focused. We bless our children when we are deliberate about our behavior toward them, expressing our love for them in particular through physical affection and verbal affirmation.

All children, whether five or fifty, need to be blessed; they need signs of love from their parents. Our family is a hugging family. Arriving and leaving are lengthy events because we take time to share hugs all around. Positive, healthy physical affection is crucial to the well-being of our children. Proverbs 3:27 says, "Do not withhold good from those who deserve it, when it is in your power to act" (NIV). Our lives are made more honorable through our liberal offer of affection to our children, whatever their age.

Verbal affirmation, equally vital, is at the heart of blessing. At the end of Genesis, Joseph hears that his father, Jacob, is dying. Joseph goes to Jacob and brings his two sons, Ephraim and Manasseh, with him.

> Then Jacob looked over at the two boys. "Are these your sons?" he asked.
> "Yes," Joseph told him, "these are the sons God has given me here in Egypt."
> And Jacob said, "Bring them over to me, and I will bless them."
> Now Jacob was half blind because of his age and could hardly see. So Joseph brought the boys close to him, and Jacob kissed and embraced them. Then Jacob said to Joseph, "I never thought I would see you again, but now God has let me see your children, too" (Gen. 48:8–11, NLT).

Jacob places his hands on Ephraim and Manasseh and offers his blessing, calling upon God to protect them and to extend to them God's promise to make them a great nation.

All children, regardless of age, long to hear their parents express love and pride and approval. Words may feel awkward, but they are powerful tools. This truth was vividly driven home to us in the recent death of our mother-in-law and grandmother, Lora Morris. Lora knew the power of blessing. She knew that her words would be held in the hearts of her family long after she was gone. Hospitalized in the aftermath of a stroke, she surely knew time was precious and she had to use it wisely, and that she did. As family gathered to be with her, she spent time with each of us, deliberately focusing on each one, sharing the strength of her faith in and love for God, her love for us. and her pride in our unique and individual accomplishments. Her words were slow and offered with great effort; not just "I love you," but "I love you very, very, very much"; the exertion involved in each "very" solidifying her blessing on each of us.

Our granddaughter and daughter, Hannah, shared a special ritual with her great-grandmother—soft kisses. When they were together, each one ever so gently touched her lips to the cheeks and lips of the other. As Lora lay in her hospital bed, Hannah offered her soft kisses. Then Lora spoke to Hannah, telling her that when she had children, she could share soft kisses with them, and then they could share them with their children and with their children and so on. "That way," she said, "my love will go on." Then she pulled Hannah close and said, "When you have something good, you need to share it."

Our children are watching us in order to find out what an honorable life looks like. Hannah was watching. When we returned home from our visit with Lora, Hannah went immediately to her room. She was there a long time. When she came out she asked for a stamp. She had a letter to send to her great-granddaddy, Gerald Morris:

Dear Granddaddy Morris:

I want to tell you to be strong. Be strong no matter what happens. Even if Grandmother Morris dies, you still need to be strong. If she does die, God will be beside her the whole way up to heaven. Then she will be watching every step you take. Also I want to tell you the whole family and I are there beside <u>you</u> every step of the way.

Love,

Hannah Reisman

P. S. You always need to keep Grandmother Morris in your heart. (I know you will.)

When you have something good, you need to share it. That was the blessing Hannah received from Lora, and through that blessing she came to know a bit more about what an honorable life actually looks like. In generously giving love and affirmation, we lay the foundation for our children's understanding of God's commandment to honor, and in doing so strengthen the bonds that bind us all to God.

REFLECTING AND RECORDING

Recall and describe an experience you shared with your parents when you felt blessed. Get in touch with as many details of the experience as possible in order to relive the blessing.

Describe a time when you sought to honor your parents by showing them how much you loved them.

What practices in your family between parents and children made you feel loved and accepted?

If you have children at home, list ongoing practices that affirm your love and acceptance of them. How did your relationship with your own parents shape these practices?

If you have adult children, are you giving them encouragement and affirmation? If they are parents, how does their relationship with their children honor you?

Look at your life in relation to your parents and their relation to you; your relationship with your children and their relation to you. How are persons spending time with one another? How are you deliberately blessing? How are you being blessed? Would a family conference about establishing more deliberate ways of relating be useful?

———— ∞∞ ————

Recall a person in your family network who especially needs to feel blessed. Name that person and pray for guidance as to how you can best communicate that blessing.

———— ∞∞ ————

DURING THE DAY

Find some way today to *bless* one or more of your children. If your parents are living, find a way to *bless* them.

DAY 6

Do Not Commit Adultery

*I*n the first four commandments, God shows us the importance of being faithful to one God, the God of Abraham, Isaac, and Jacob. In the seventh commandment, "You shall not commit adultery" (Exod. 20:14), God expresses the importance of being faithful to one mate, a marriage partner. Faithfulness in each of these arenas of life is intimately connected to the other.

The connection between relationship with God and relationship with a spouse is evident in the words describing both. We are a holy people because of our relationship with God. In Deuteronomy we read, "For you are a holy people, who belong to the LORD your God. Of all the people on earth, the LORD your God has chosen you to be his own special treasure" (Deut. 7:6, NLT). The Hebrew words for "engaged" (*kiddushin*) and "marriage" (*nisuin*) also point to the holy nature of the marital relationship. *Kiddushin* is related to the Hebrew word *kadosh,* meaning "holy" or "set aside for a godly purpose." Thus, when a couple decides to marry, each person takes the first step in setting the relationship with future spouse aside for a godly purpose; this promise becomes a sacred covenant paralleling the covenantal relationship between God and God's people. The step beyond engagement, marriage itself, is referred to in Hebrew as *nisuin,* meaning "uplifting." When a couples enters into a holy relationship similar to relationship with God, their marriage relationship is elevated to a sanctified level.

The connection between faithfulness to God and faithfulness to spouse is seen not only in the words used to describe these relationships. God actually uses the marriage relationship as a metaphor for God's relationship with us. God tells the prophet Hosea, "I will take you [Israel] for my wife forever; I will take you for my wife in righteousness and in justice, in steadfast love, and in mercy. I will take you for my wife in faithfulness; and you shall *know* the LORD" (Hos. 2:19-20, emphasis added).

Our faithfulness to each other affects our faithfulness to God.

The key to this metaphor is the word *know.* I can recall as a teenager giggling with my friends in church when the preacher would read, "Now the man knew his wife Eve . . ." (Gen. 4:1). We all understood what that word meant: Adam had had sexual intercourse with Eve. Describing sexual intimacy in this way is significant. From a biblical perspective, sex is a sacred act, occurring when two people know each other and recognize their sexual union as part of a holy relationship. Comparing the divine-human relationship to marriage points to this type of knowing. We can see the connection between faithfulness to God and faithfulness to spouse when we recognize that knowing God and knowing a spouse both require comprehending the type of commitment involved as well as the energy necessary to nourish the relationship. Spiritual estrangement—from each other and from God—occurs when two people do not share this awareness and deeper sense of knowing.

The story of Hosea vividly illustrates the link between fidelity to God and fidelity in marriage. It is a story of pain, the pain of adultery and faithlessness. God instructs Hosea to marry Gomer, despite the fact that she is a prostitute and therefore would have difficulty identifying the father of her children. As the story unfolds, Hosea's pain at his wife's betrayal mirrors God's pain, caused by the Israelites' unfaithfulness. Yet, by the end of the book, compassion and hope emerge for both relationships. In the story of Hosea we recognize that what we do in relationship with our spouse holds significance beyond ourselves. Our faithfulness to each other affects our faithfulness to God.

To begin to understand God's commandment against adultery, we must first appreciate the significance of the marriage relationship itself and its intimate connection to our relationship with God. Marriage is a holy relationship even as our relationship with God is holy. Marriage sanctifies our human need for companionship. Practicing fidelity in the marriage relationship provides experience in being faithful in relationship with God and, conversely, faithfulness in relating to God reinforces commitment to fidelity in marriage.

There can be no doubt about the strong connection between fidelity to God and fidelity in marriage. Therefore, there can be no doubt about the seriousness of God's commandment against adultery. Throughout the Old Testament, adultery symbolizes the broken faith of God's chosen people. "How can I pardon you?" God asks Israel through the prophet Jeremiah. "For even your children have turned from me. They have sworn by gods that are not gods at all! I fed my people until they were fully satisfied. But they thanked me by committing adultery and lining up at the city's brothels" (Jer. 5:7, NLT).

The seventh commandment concerns not only our relationship with our spouse but our relationship with God. We have one mate as we have one God. Ultimately, in showing faithfulness to our mate, we show faithfulness to God. Conversely, when we fall short in faithfulness to our spouse, we also fall short in faithfulness to God.

REFLECTING AND RECORDING

Spend a few minutes reflecting on the following ideas:

Marriage is a relationship of a man and a woman set aside for a godly purpose.

———— ❧ ————

God uses marriage as a metaphor for the relationship between God and persons because faithfulness is required in both relationships.

———— ❧ ————

Practicing fidelity in a marriage relationship provides us experience in being faithful in our relationship with God.

———— ❧ ————

Our faithfulness in relating to God reinforces our commitment to fidelity in marriage.

DURING THE DAY

Seek an opportunity to engage someone in a conversation about marriage as a metaphor for our relationship with God.

If you know someone who is suffering because a spouse has been unfaithful, pray for that person; also seek the opportunity to encourage and support that person in his/her faithfulness.

DAY 7

Love, a Matter of Will;
Marriage, a Matter of Commitment

> It was also said, "Whoever divorces his wife, let him give her a certificate of divorce." But I say to you that anyone who divorces his wife, except on the ground of unchastity, causes her to commit adultery; and whoever marries a divorced woman commits adultery.—Matthew 5:31-32

C. L. Null was teaching a Sunday school class of first graders about the Ten Commandments. When the class reached the seventh commandment, "Do not commit adultery," a little girl raised her hand and asked, "What does *commit* mean?" (www.PreachingToday.com 2/9/02).

What does commit *mean?* That seems to be the heart of our trouble with the seventh commandment. We don't appear to understand commitment. In an essay entitled "The Loves," Sheldon Vanauken describes conversations with two Christian friends who each had left their spouse for another. One said, "It seemed so good, so right. That's when we knew we had to get the divorces. We belonged together." The other expressed similar feelings, "It was just so good and right with Roger that I knew it would be wrong to go on with Paul." Vanauken explains that rather than adhering to the law of fidelity and commitment, we invoke what is for us a higher law: "the feeling of goodness and rightness . . . a feeling so powerful that it [sweeps] away . . . whatever guilt [we] would otherwise [feel]" for what we are doing to our marriages and our families (www.PreachingToday.com 2/09/02).

It is sad but true that our society emphasizes the self over everything else. We hear that our individual feelings are paramount and that we must "do what feels right for us." We continually redefine morality, not in ways that strengthen our moral backbone but in ways that lower the common denominator, moving us toward an accommodating, nonjudgmental, self-governing, and self-centered path. We are less and less willing to make any kind of judgment about sexual behavior unless, of course, we are an injured party. Rather than seriously addressing the importance of being monogamous, we lightheartedly compare it to losing weight—we know we should do it, but most of us lack the willpower.

Our lenient attitude in the area of faithfulness points to a tendency for hypocrisy as well as a gross misunderstanding of the meaning of commitment. Our hypocrisy reveals itself in efforts to rationalize our betrayal while we, of course, don't want to be betrayed. Our misunderstanding of commitment derives from following society's emphasis on feelings rather than recognizing that commitment involves the will. When we make a commitment, all our subsequent behavior stems from the deliberate decision to keep that commitment, regardless of what our feelings tell us. This is not to deny enormous temptations, times when feelings are so strong it seems impossible not to follow them. Yet true commitment entails the ability to look beyond our feelings to the feelings of the one to whom we are committed, to put ourselves in that person's position.

God does not intend brokenness in families. God desires wholeness—the security of commitment, of promises kept, of trust. The seventh commandment, against adultery, is the means for protecting that wholeness and security. In keeping the commandment, we assure not only our own wholeness but the wholeness of those who trust us as well.

REFLECTING AND RECORDING

If you are married and have been able to sustain fidelity in your marriage; or, if your marriage has survived infidelity, write a prayer of confession and thanksgiving for God's faithfulness and the presence of Christ in your relationship.

Facts being what they are—that in 80 percent of marriages, one partner or the other will be unfaithful—you may have been the unfaithful one. Confess your unfaithfulness to the Lord. How are you seeking the Lord's strength and the support of a Christian fellowship to stay faithful?

In what ways are you carrying a burden of guilt and shame for past sexual sins? Remember the story of the woman caught in adultery who was brought to Jesus for judgment. "Neither do I condemn you," Jesus said, "go and sin no more" (John 8:11, NKJV). Write a prayer of confession and repentance; express your willingness to receive Christ's forgiveness.

Make a list of persons you know whose marriages are threatened because of adultery. Commit yourself to praying for those persons and supporting them in whatever way possible.

If you are in an adulterous relationship, acknowledge the sin and destructiveness of it, find the help you need to get out of that relationship, and recover your faithfulness to God and to your spouse.

————⊗⊗⊗————

DURING THE DAY

Begin praying for and ministering to the people you listed above.

Group Meeting for Week Five

INTRODUCTION

In group sharing it is essential that each person practice the disciplines of intention and attention. It is easy to take the lazy route in group participation—to be more passive than active. Group members may be tempted to "play it safe" and not risk involvement, honesty, and vulnerability.

Energy is another issue. Listening and speaking demand physical as well as emotional energy. So the temptation is to hold back, to be only half-present, not to invest the attention and focus essential for full participation.

We urge you to withstand these temptations. These sharing sessions are important. Don't underestimate the value of each person's contribution. Stay sensitive to the possibility of sliding into laziness.

SHARING TOGETHER

1. Begin your time together with prayer led by the group leader or someone else (consulted ahead of time). Then sing a chorus or a couple of stanzas of a hymn everyone knows.

2. Ask each person to share the most challenging and meaningful insight or experience gained during this week.

3. Spend five to eight minutes discussing the biblical meaning of *honor*. How is this different from the way you have understood the commandment "Honor your father and your mother"? What is the difference between love and honor?

4. Spend ten to twelve minutes exploring the connection between the command for children to obey their parents and the possibility of making idols of our children (which we considered in Week 3). Did the way your parents required obedience shape you positively or negatively?

5. Invite a couple of people to share their responses to this statement: Parents are to be to their children what God is to the world.

6. Spend eight to ten minutes discussing three aspects of honoring our parents (Day 4):

   • courteous behavior

   • recognizing significance

   • acceptance

7. Discuss the connection between the call of God in the first commandment (You shall have no other gods before me) and the faithfulness called for in the seventh commandment (You shall not commit adultery). How is marriage a metaphor for God's relationship with us?

8. Invite two or three persons to share their responses to this statement: Marriage is a relationship of a man and woman set aside for a godly purpose.

9. *Leader:* Ask the group if there are issues, concerns, or questions related to the week that may need attention. Spend what time you have left dealing with these.

PRAYING TOGETHER

William Law said, "Praying is not speaking forth eloquently, but simply, the true desire of the heart" (Law, *Works of the Reverend William Law,* vol. 7, 132). Remember this as you enter this period of prayer.

1. Begin with a period of silent prayer, holding before God in loving concern the persons in your groups, specifically what they have shared in this session and in previous weeks. Take three or four minutes for this silent prayer.

2. Now enter a period of "conversational prayer" when persons offer brief prayers growing out of this session's sharing. The prayers of one may prompt the praying of another. Persons should feel free to pray "more than once"—simply lifting to the Lord the concerns that come to mind as the prayer time progresses. Don't let any need or concern shared in this session go unprayed for. Don't rush. Take as much time as needed.

3. To close, let one person offer a prayer aloud on behalf of the group for the families represented in the group.

4. Don't forget to exchange "prayer photos."

R*everence for Human Life*

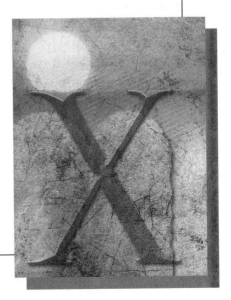

DAY 1
The Sacredness of Human Life

*T*he sixth, seventh, and eighth commandments are expressed in only two words each in Hebrew. They could be paraphrased simply: "No killing, no adultery, no stealing." Put positively, these commandments call us to reverence human life and to respect the rights of others. The foundation for the sixth commandment is in the Creation story, in which God made us in God's own likeness. Humankind is of infinite value to the Creator.

Life is sacred because it is the gift of God. We characterize and evaluate people by many methods and with many labels: intellect and education, financial and social positions. However we identify people, and we do—by nationality and race, by political positions, by economic status—the bottom line is this: Life is the gift of God.

> Then God said, "Let us make humankind in our image, according to our likeness; and let them have dominion over the fish of the sea, and over the birds of the air, and over the cattle, and over all the wild animals of the earth, and over every creeping thing that creeps upon the earth."
>   So God created humankind in his image,/in the image of God he created them;/male and female he created them (Gen. 1:26-27).

Life is sacred because of its God-given purpose. We were made for a relationship with God, created to know and love God, to express the likeness of God in our living. A major and distinctive characteristic of our uniqueness as human beings is our ability to communicate with God and to be communicated to by God. Our communication potential with God will find its fulfillment only in eternity, where, with all the redeemed, we will share God's glory and worship God forever. Because of the Fall and our fall, our relationship with God has been broken, and we cannot fulfill our capacity to express God's likeness. God comes to remedy that situation in Jesus Christ, in whom we witness the full meaning of humanity's sacredness. Jesus' death and resurrection restore our broken relationship with God. *Life is sacred because God has redeemed life.*

Of all the commandments, the sixth—do not murder—seems to be the easiest to dismiss as not being connected to the realm of our daily life. For the vast majority, murder is something we encounter on the news or in novels and movies but not in everyday living. Yet at the heart of this commandment lies a notion relevant to us as individuals and as a society. The Hebrew word used in the sixth commandment is *tirtzach*, which reflects wrongful killing. The English word *murder* accurately conveys the sense of wrongfulness, yet at the same time it removes the act from our daily lives. This sense of wrongfulness, however, is the very thing that makes the commandment relevant to daily life. *Wrongful killing*, not only murder as we see it portrayed in newspapers and mystery novels, is what God prohibits in the sixth commandment.

We are not just a highly developed, complex bundle of cells. Unlike all other creatures on earth, we are tied to God because God breathed God's own Spirit into us to give us life. Since

God formed us and gave us life, only God has the right to determine when that life will end. The ending of life is God's domain. When we intentionally do take a life, we are "playing God" and commandeering God's authority.

REFLECTING AND RECORDING

Spend a few minutes reflecting and make some notes on each of the reasons human life is sacred:

- Life is sacred because it is the gift of God.

- Life is sacred because of its God-given purpose.

- Life is sacred because God has redeemed life.

DURING THE DAY

Keep a record of how many times you encounter "murder" today—in the newspaper, on TV, in conversation, in your reading. Ask yourself: What is the possible cause for this destruction of life?

 DAY 2
Usurping God's Authority

Disobedience to the sixth commandment is regarded as a sign of a depraved society in scripture. The prophet Hosea complains, "Hear the word of the LORD, O people of Israel;/for the LORD has an indictment against the inhabitants of the land./There is no faithfulness or loyalty,/and no knowledge of God in the land./Swearing, lying, and murder,/and stealing and adultery break out;/bloodshed follows bloodshed" (Hos. 4:1-2).

Loving our neighbors as ourselves and doing to others what we would have them do to us are helpful in establishing social order. Yet that social order means little in the face of gang violence or terrorist acts in which the perpetrators do not care about dying themselves. If murder is wrong simply because society has laid down laws to that effect, then we will have great difficulty dealing with a society such as Nazi Germany where killing Jews, Gypsies, homosexuals, the severely retarded, and any other group of individuals deemed inferior was officially sanctioned by the government and tacitly accepted by German society. If Holocaust history seems too far in the past, recall the horror of "ethnic cleansing" in Bosnia or the genocide in Rwanda.

The commandment not to kill more sharply polarizes the thinking of Christians than any other.

The objective reality is that murder is wrong, not because society has laws to that effect but because murder violates the sanctity of life and usurps God's authority to determine when life will end. Allen Redpath reminds us that "this commandment, in a very simple way and yet in a most definite language, flings a wall of fire around every human being and reserves to God, who first gave life, the right to end it. For the one relationship which death does not end is man's relationship to God. He has a purpose for every individual, each one of us, to be recognized here in time and realized in eternity. The issues of death are so great because of this fact that there could be no greater sin against humanity or against God than the taking of life. It is said, 'Life is cheap,' but God says that life is sacred" (Redpath, *Law and Liberty*, 69).

In the Old Testament we read that God delegated to the Hebrew nation the right to maintain God's law and righteousness. Under the code of defined conditions laid down by God, killing was acceptable only if a person acted as an agent of God's righteousness to rid the land of evil. In the New Testament application of this law, as with the application of other laws, the ministry, life, and teaching of Jesus magnify all the commandments and God's intention for humankind. Jesus made it clear that he had not come to destroy the law but to fulfill it. While killing was seen in the Old Testament as an instrument of God's judgment, Jesus rebuked James and John for attempting to call down fire from heaven upon those who refused to hear him (Luke 9:55). When Peter made a desperate effort to stop Jesus' arrest, Jesus said to him, "Put your sword back into its place; for all who take the sword will perish by the sword" (Matt. 26:52). When bystanders reminded Jesus that the penalty for the woman caught in adultery was death by stoning, Jesus challenged those who were without sin to throw the first stone. No one responded, and Jesus said to the woman, "Neither do I condemn you. Go your way, and from now on do not sin again" (John 8:11).

The commandment not to kill more sharply polarizes the thinking of Christians than any other. Contemporary issues associated with this commandment—abortion, euthanasia, war, the death penalty—create barriers that divide families, friends, even churches. Many times we don't even know how to have a conversation about them. As we think about these issues, we must take care not to demonize persons who think differently than we, remembering that compassionate and caring people of faith can hold different opinions on these issues. Of course, some of these issues will be impossible to resolve completely this side of eternity.

We need to consider the possibility that there are more sacred things in life than "the sacredness of life." In the Christian view of reality, truth is more sacred than life itself. Through the ages,

Christians have died rather than surrender the authority of truth. As modern Christians we must ask ourselves whether there may be occasions when life should be surrendered in order that the true worth and dignity of persons is preserved.

REFLECTING AND RECORDING

We will consider capital punishment, euthanasia, abortion, and war over the next four days. With those four issues in mind, spend a few minutes reflecting on this statement: Murder is wrong because it violates the sanctity of life and usurps God's authority to determine when life will end.

———— ⬦⬦⬦ ————

In the Old Testament, God used persons and nations as agents of God's judgment. In what ways do you see that happening today?

———— ⬦⬦⬦ ————

If you are using this workbook in a group, think of the persons in your group. Try to imagine the diversity of opinion among them. Pray that your discussion of the issues related to killing will not be divisive, that persons will listen and respect one another.

———— ⬦⬦⬦ ————

Recall a person who suffered because of his or her loyalty to Christ. Name and describe that person's experience.

———— ⬦⬦⬦ ————

In light of this person's loyalty and willingness to suffer, explore your own commitment. Are you willing to suffer for your loyalty to Christ?

———— ⬦⬦⬦ ————

Spend the balance of your time reflecting on this claim: My life is not as sacred as my self.

———— ⬦⬦⬦ ————

DURING THE DAY

Write or call the person you named who has suffered for loyalty to Christ. Express your appreciation for the power of his or her witness.

DAY 3
Capital Punishment

*P*art of our kingdom work as Christians involves bringing our faith to bear on a variety of issues currently facing our country, including the debate over the death penalty. Our country executes more people today than at any other time in our history. We must search the Bible, study Christian tradition, explore our experience of the Holy Spirit, and use the powers of reason God has given us in order to understand God's will regarding the death penalty. This is not an easy task, as the Bible can be used to support both sides of the question. Not surprisingly, few thinking people can avoid a struggle with this issue.

In a commandment even older than the law given to Moses, God tells Noah: "Murder is forbidden. Animals that kill people must die, and any person who murders must be killed. Yes, you must execute anyone who murders another person, for to kill a person is to kill a living being made in God's image" (Gen. 9:5-6, NLT). God commands that a murderer should be put to death. This directive clearly supports the idea of the death penalty and was meant to deter people from murdering.

Throughout the Old Testament similar passages support the concept of the death penalty, with distinctions between manslaughter and murder. These laws all rested on the belief that God values each human life and that God alone has the right to determine when life will end.

In contrast to its function in modern society, the death penalty played a key role in maintaining social order and deterring violence. At the time these laws were given, the Israelites were a nomadic people, wandering the wilderness without the benefit of a criminal justice system, police force, or prisons. For a nomadic people living in tents, "life in prison without parole" was not an option. The death penalty was the only way to assure that a murderer or other criminal would not hurt others again.

As the primary means of maintaining order, the death penalty was the punishment for numerous sins, not just murder. Sixteen crimes were punishable by death, including disobedience or disrespect of parents, working on the sabbath, and sexual activity outside marriage. Despite the fact that the Old Testament supports capital punishment, few desire to use it in the manner in which it was used during that time. In fact, few of us would be alive today if we were subject to Old Testament standards.

The New Testament provides a radically different perspective on God and humanity. Jesus, through his life, death, and resurrection, consistently conveys a message of mercy. Rather than elaborating on the principle of "an eye for an eye," Jesus lived out the concept of mercy. When confronted with the woman caught in adultery, rather than approving the lawful sentence of death by stoning, Jesus showed mercy. Hanging on the cross, Jesus responded with mercy to the plea of a criminal who might have been a murderer.

As Paul says, "All have sinned; all fall short of God's glorious standard" (Rom. 3:23, NLT). Scripture tells us that all of us have been sentenced to death under the law. If we have not violated the letter of the Ten Commandments, which many of us have, we have violated the spirit and the intention of the law.

The good news of Jesus Christ, however, is that we have received God's mercy! Our sin was nailed to a cross and our salvation assured. Certainly consequences of sin remain, but it seems uncomfortably hypocritical to support the death penalty for others without offering hope of redemption or mercy, standing as we do only by the grace and mercy of God. We may be proponents of the death penalty because we desire retribution in response to evil, yet we, sinful as we are, have received grace instead of retribution.

Recall that Paul was first Saul, the archenemy of the early church, the one who both blessed and witnessed the stoning of Stephen. If there were ever someone who deserved the death penalty, it was Paul. Justice would demand a sentence of death. Instead, God broke into Paul's life in a dramatic and life-changing way, bringing him to acceptance of Christ as his Lord, to a life of great peril and sacrifice. Paul deserved death, but through the death of Jesus received God's mercy.

> How thankful I am to Christ Jesus our Lord for considering me trustworthy and appointing me to serve him, even though I used to scoff at the name of Christ. I hunted down his people, harming them in every way I could. But God had mercy on me because I did it in ignorance and unbelief (1 Tim. 1:12-13, NLT).

According to the scriptures, each of us deserves the death penalty; yet God, so rich in mercy, determined that there would be another way, an atoning sacrifice that would be made on our behalf. Jesus, God incarnate, was that sacrifice.

The sixth commandment demands that we remember God is the only One with rightful authority to take life. Does acceptance and promotion of capital punishment contradict the very gospel we proclaim as Christians?

REFLECTING AND RECORDING

Review today's content, making notes of any new thoughts or insights about capital punishment. Record those here.

If you have disagreements with what we have said about capital punishment, write those here.

Spend the balance of your time reflecting on this disconnect: While we deserve death for our sins, Christ shows us mercy; at the same time, many of us believe that those who murder should be killed in retribution for their acts.

DURING THE DAY

If you know someone who is in prison, write him or her a note of encouragement. Or, if you know someone who ministers to prisoners, write or call with a word of encouragement.

Engage someone in conversation today, asking for a response to what we have said about capital punishment.

DAY 4
Euthanasia

> That is why we never give up. Though our bodies are dying, our spirits are being renewed every day. For our present troubles are quite small and won't last very long. Yet they produce for us an immeasurably great glory that will last forever! So we don't look at the troubles we can see right now; rather, we look forward to what we have not yet seen. For the troubles we see will soon be over, but the joys to come will last forever.—2 Corinthians 4:16-18, NLT

*A*cross the country every day, real-life scenarios unfold, necessitating complicated and painful decisions about medical treatment for the dying. As Christians we need to understand God's will regarding death and human suffering and be clear about acceptable and unacceptable ways to care for the dying.

The concept of euthanasia has been around for a long time, but in recent years the efforts of Dr. Jack Kevorkian brought the issue to national attention and generated heated debate. Literally meaning "good death," the word *euthanasia* in our culture has come to mean "mercy killing" or ending a person's life in order to assuage suffering. Two other concepts are often associated with the idea of mercy killing—"the right to die" and "death with dignity." As individuals receive medical treatment in the course of serious physical crises, artificial means of life support such as respirators, ventilators, or heart machines may become necessary. In many cases these machines can be withdrawn successfully when the crisis has passed; however, sometimes an irreversible condition leaves family members grappling with the decision of whether to withdraw life support and face a loved one's inevitable death. These various end-of-life issues came under scrutiny when Dr. Kevorkian promoted a form of euthanasia known as "physician-assisted suicide." In this protocol, a physician could hasten a patient's death by prescribing lethal medication to be self-administered or by administering the medication if the patient were no longer capable.

Most ethicists agree that the key distinction between withdrawal of life support and euthanasia is the difference between omission and commission. When we remove a patient from life-support devices, we recognize that the individual is dying and will not be able to sustain life apart from artificial means. Guidelines to ensure that the withdrawal of life support is morally acceptable include the following:

- All treatments likely to restore health have been exhausted.
- The patient has entered the death process and will die without life support.
- The patient will not recover; therefore, life support only postpones the inevitable.
- The patient does not want to be kept alive by artificial means.

When these conditions have been met, we can confidently withdraw life support without fearing that we are responsible for another's death. While removing life support may speed the patient's death, it is not our action but the physical condition or disease that causes death.

Just as withholding extraordinary life support is not euthanasia, neither is a person's refusal to receive medical care for a particular illness. Euthanasia is the direct taking of life, another's or one's own, in order to alleviate suffering. Supporters of euthanasia often say there is little distinction between allowing someone to die and helping them to die; they believe euthanasia to be the humane alternative to facing frightening, incapacitating, and painful illnesses.

As compelling and compassionate as the argument in favor of euthanasia may be, alternative methods can alleviate or significantly reduce pain. Hospice care is a remarkable support for families managing the needs of their dying loved ones. The sterile nature of Dr. Kevorkian's crusade for euthanasia stands in stark contrast to death experiences we have been blessed to witness. Far from being alone, these persons were surrounded by friends and/or family. They fought their illnesses and medical circumstances with courage until there was no hope for recovery. When it became clear that death was inevitable, they placed themselves in God's care as they had throughout their lives. Often they put forth a great deal of effort to share their love with and receive love from their families. Their pain was eased with medication and when the time was right, they stopped fighting—eating less and sleeping more—until finally they began to sleep into death. As Adam Hamilton has said, "God has the power to stop our heart from beating when it is our time. God doesn't need our help in the process" (Hamilton, *Confronting the Controversies*, 73).

Christianity teaches that life is a gift from God, a gift that includes each day of our lives. Our bodies belong to God and are part of that gift of life as well. When we choose to end life before God's time, we are rejecting God's gift and maybe even God the Giver as well.

As Christians, we believe that God can use our suffering for good—our own good and that of others. While for those who support euthanasia, suffering is a great evil to be avoided, suffering is not an enemy of those who follow Christ. Jesus understood suffering; he experienced it before his death, and he even prayed that it might be taken away from him. Yet even as he asked God to take suffering away from him, Jesus put God's destiny for him before his own desires. Our response to suffering is a commitment to God's power to bring good out of evil and tragedy.

So how do we respond to suffering and death in this debate about euthanasia? First, we remember the healing ministry of Jesus, who said that one of the criteria used at the Last Judgment would be our care of the sick (Matt. 25:36). As followers of Christ we are to carry on his ministry through our own care, with mercy and understanding, of those who are suffering, in pain, or facing devastating medical situations.

Second, we respond to this debate by remembering what the gospel says about confronting suffering and death: God carries us. No matter what our circumstances, we face them with the hope that God will never abandon us. Each gospel story works its way toward one moment in time: the brutal, pain-filled death of Jesus on the cross. But even that is not the end of the story. The power of the gospel message comes with the Resurrection, the victory of Jesus Christ over suffering and death.

In the debate over euthanasia, the world needs to see how Christians face death and suffering: knowing that our lives are not our own, that they belong to Christ; believing that because God has the authority to decide when life ends, God will call us home in God's own time, not in ours; hoping that God's light and love can shine through us—even through our suffering—and that God can use us to bring good out of evil.

Adam Hamilton says, "The real dignity in death comes from those who walk with Christ to the very last day, those who, especially in the face of suffering, let Christ shine through them and then listen for his voice as he calls them home" (*Confronting the Controversies*, 77). As Christians, that is the only way to face death—by allowing God to use us, even in our dying, to bear witness to God's love in the world.

REFLECTING AND RECORDING

Review today's reading, making notes of any new thoughts or insights about euthanasia.

If you have disagreements about what we have said about euthanasia, record those here.

Recall the suffering and death of someone you have known. How did the person deal with pain and suffering? What helpful lessons did you learn from the person about facing your own suffering and death? What role did the person's faith play in the way he or she faced death?

Recall and record here an experience when God used your suffering for your good or the good of others; or, record the experience of someone you know whose suffering God used for that person's good or the good of others.

Spend the balance of your time thinking about what "a good death" or "death with dignity" means to you.

DURING THE DAY

If you know someone facing death, struggling with the death of a loved one, or debating the question of removing life support, call or write that person a note of encouragement.

Engage someone in conversation today about euthanasia.

DAY 5
Abortion

> You made all the delicate, inner parts of my body
>   and knit me together in my mother's womb.
> Thank you for making me so wonderfully complex!
>   Your workmanship is marvelous—and how well I know it.
> You watched me as I was being formed in utter seclusion,
>   as I was woven together in the dark of the womb.
> You saw me before I was born.
>   Every day of my life was recorded in your book.
> Every moment was laid out
>   before a single day had passed.—Psalm 139:13-16, NLT

*F*ew moral issues facing society today are as controversial or emotionally charged as abortion. No matter which side of the issue people find themselves on, emotions can rapidly raise the discussion to a fever pitch. As Christians we bring our biblical and theological resources to bear on this divisive issue in order to find clarity for ourselves in the midst of the debate.

If you did not live through the 1960s and 1970s, it may be difficult to comprehend the extent of upheaval and change that occurred during those decades. Traditional values about sexual behavior were called into question. Women were demonstrating for civil rights with a new assertiveness and urgency. There was serious discussion about what rights women have to control their own bodies. It was truly a time of immense social revolution.

In the midst of this tumultuous social climate, in 1973, the Supreme Court ruled in the now-famous *Roe v. Wade* abortion case. At the time of the ruling, abortion was illegal in forty-six states. Thus, when the Supreme Court agreed with Jane Roe's attorneys that abortion laws were unconstitutional based on the Ninth and the Fourteenth amendments, its ruling resulted in dismay, outrage, and bitterness among its foes.

Much has been said about the court's ruling in the years since it was handed down. Many believe the court should have allowed the people and states to work through the issue. Although court actions in the years since the Roe decision have allowed states to add certain stipulations to first-trimester abortions such as waiting periods and parental consent for minors, the first result was that abortion on demand was instantly available in all fifty states. Second, rather than the anticipated 400,000–500,000 legal abortions per year, 744,600 were performed in 1973 and 898,600 in 1974. That number had grown to over 1,600,000 per year by 1990. While that number has declined slightly—approximately 1,300,000 abortions were performed in 1998—over 38 million abortions have been performed in the U.S. in the years since *Roe v. Wade.*

Compassionate and committed Christians on both sides navigate these often turbulent waters, earnestly claiming Jesus as Lord and holding carefully thought-out opinions that differ. Let us explore how this difference is possible.

No one we know supports abortion because they believe it is a good thing. Many who would not personally have an abortion believe there are situations so traumatic that a woman should have the right not to have the child. Deep shame still accompanies having a baby out of wedlock for many. The struggle to raise a child alone is immense. The mental anguish of carrying a baby for nine months, bearing that child, and then giving him or her up for adoption is enormous.

The situations leading to a woman's decision to terminate a pregnancy are often complex. Women are pressured into sex by boyfriends. The fathers of the unborn frequently abandon pregnant women. Poverty or drugs may complicate the situation; rape, incest, or the discovery of genetic defects dramatically increases the complexity of a woman's decision. Choices of this nature are never clear-cut, and not a few people who opposed abortion have changed their opinions when faced with the pregnancy of a teenage daughter or knowledge of inevitable birth defects. Christians who support abortion usually do so out of a deep concern for the plight of the women who face such overwhelming circumstances and the future of the unborn.

Compassion also motivates most Christians who oppose abortions. Certainly there are extremists who act out of anger and hatred. However, they do not represent most Christians who believe abortion is wrong, who also have great concern for the well-being of women, often supporting such services as crisis pregnancy centers, mentoring ministries for unwed mothers, or residential programs for pregnant teens.

Christians opposing abortion point out that conception and the development of life in the months following are miraculous and sacred. Modern medicine confirms the awe-inspiring nature of developing life in the womb, belying the assertion that what lies within is mere "tissue." Before the end of the first trimester, the unborn child is a miniature human being with eyes, ears, mouth, toes, and fingers. The unborn suck thumbs and move around; they respond to noise. Christians opposing abortion often ask why we call a wanted child a baby while it is yet unborn, but the unwanted child is referred to as a fetus. They emphasize that it is the same child whether we desire it or reject it.

Christians who oppose abortion believe all life is a gift from God and that only God has the right to determine when it will end. They often highlight the unspoken price women pay when they have an abortion, an emotional toll that many women discover only after the fact. In stressing God's gift of life, these Christians emphasize that abortion cannot be condensed to a "choice" or to the termination of a "pregnancy." Rather, it ends a life, stops a heart, destroys a brain.

What does the Bible actually *say* about abortion? Nothing directly; however, there are passages that can inform our understanding. Genesis 9:5-6 clearly places determining the end of life outside our realm of control. Psalm 139 and Jeremiah 1:5 describe God's work within the womb, knitting us together, knowing who we will be, shaping our character, molding our abilities, creating our physical features. Paul writes that our bodies are not our own but are gifts from God (1 Cor. 6:19-20). John, the unborn child of Elizabeth, leaps in his mother's womb at the sound of Mary's voice in Luke 1. Mary is carrying the unborn child Jesus in her own womb when she greets her cousin Elizabeth. God chose an unwed teenage girl to birth the Savior of the world. God takes the unexpected, the painful, the complicated, the seemingly insurmountable situations in our lives and uses them for God's purpose.

Compassionate and committed Christians on both sides navigate these often turbulent waters.

It is easy to keep the abortion debate in the realm of the hypothetical, but if we do so, we risk missing what lies at the heart of the discussion: real persons—real women who face painful decisions; real children, as yet unborn, whose lives hang in the balance. Real-life stories reveal women who as teenagers found themselves doctor's offices where their tears elicited only gruff referrals to abortion clinics and the words "This is what you need to do . . ."; women who cried secret tears alone, stunned and confused at emotional turmoil for which no one prepared them; women for whom time has eased pain, yet who can tell you, years later, the age their aborted child would be had their decision been different.

We know the stories of other women: women who longed for children of their own but could never have them; women who contemplated ending their pregnancies but chose instead to deliver their babies, only to place them into the loving and longing arms of another woman; college women whose boyfriends abandoned them upon learning of their pregnancies but whose families supported them as they brought their infants to us for baptism.

We know the stories of children as well. In a letter to her son, one woman wrote:

Yes, my life changed dramatically due to the pregnancy prior to marriage, but to this day, that child has been the greatest blessing to me and thousands of others . . . God has blessed me more with this son than I can ever imagine being blessed. . . . Thank you, Adam, for being my "gift from God." There can be no greater gift than that of a child that God wants to be born (Hamilton, *Confronting the Controversies*, 106-7).

In his book *Confronting the Controversies*, Adam Hamilton shared that letter and continued:

This is *my* story, and this letter was written by my mother. And what it reminds me of is a powerful gospel truth: God takes what we think of as "mistakes," "accidents," and "blunders," and redeems them. This is God's specialty. God knits us together in our mothers' wombs and has plans for each child. God can work—sometimes through birth parents, sometimes through wonderful adoptive parents who could never have a child of their own. But those children have potential. They grow up. I am one of those children (Hamilton, *Confronting the Controversies*, 107).

As we struggle with this heart-wrenching issue, we must remember that our God is a God of grace who understands our pain and knows the burdens we carry. We may need to come before God with the burden of our past. We may need to come before God with the challenges of our future. In either case, we come knowing that God desires nothing more than to forgive us, to wipe every tear from our eyes, to embrace us and make us whole. Proverbs 3:5-8 instructs us to trust in God with all our heart and not to rely on our own insight. Paul reminds us to pray without ceasing (1 Thess. 5:17). Knowing that God has a future and a hope laid out for us to claim enables us to face this issue with wisdom and determination, looking forward to healing for our past and strength for our future.

REFLECTING AND RECORDING

For Men
Has a woman pregnant with your baby had an abortion, or do you have a female friend who has had an abortion? Make some notes describing the circumstances, your response, the woman's response, and the emotional result of the abortion. How do you feel now about the abortion?

For Women
Have you or a friend had an abortion? Make some notes about the circumstances, the emotional result, and how you presently feel about the abortion.

Would you describe yourself using either current term "pro-life" or "pro-choice"? Write some notes about your response.

If you have received any new insight or information from the discussion of abortion, note how your thinking about abortion may be affected.

Spend the balance of your time considering what churches or special interest or ministry groups in your community are doing about the abortion issue. Are you engaged in Christian dialogue and ministry around this difficult issue in your community?

DURING THE DAY

If you know anyone pregnant out of wedlock who has decided against abortion or someone who has had an abortion recently, pray for that woman; where appropriate, write or call her to offer love and support.

Today seek to engage in conversation a person who has strong convictions on this issue.

 DAY 6
A Middle Way

*A*s we write this, American troops have engaged in a full-scale war in Iraq and are now shouldering the difficult responsibility of keeping peace. This war was generally supported in the United States but has created a great deal of debate. One of the most troubling questions for us as we look at the sixth commandment is, *What is the Christian response to war?* The issue of "just war" has been debated vigorously over the years. What does it mean for a war to be just?

The idea originated with Augustine and was expanded by Thomas Aquinas in the thirteenth century when he formulated three basic conditions that must be met for a "just war." First, the war must be waged by the appropriate authority, such as our secular government. Second, the cause itself must be just. In other words, we must be confident we are participating in a war that is a "necessary evil" in order to accomplish a "greater good." Finally, we must fight with the idea of establishing the "greater good" or bringing an end to a great evil.

The just-war formulation has worked well in the past. In World War II, for instance, it was clear that freedom and democracy were greater goods worthy of fighting for and protecting, while the fascism and genocide promoted by the Nazis were tremendous evils that needed to be eliminated. Unfortunately the war on terrorism is not nearly as easy to sort out; nor was the war in Iraq. Certainly terrorism is a great evil that needs to be eliminated; however, the means for eliminating it are not as clear-cut as the options were during World War II. With whom we align ourselves and against whom we fight are not self-evident, since the enemy in a war on terrorism could be anywhere, and, being sinful human beings, our own motives are not always as pure as we would wish.

When someone has attacked us, hurt us, or threatened us, we desire retribution. The desire for revenge often stems from our inclination to divide the world into two parts: the forces of evil (usually a power other than ourselves) and the forces of good (usually whatever side we are on). In our current situation, the forces of evil are presented as Iraq (for harboring and promoting terrorism) and the larger Islamic terrorist network. We regard the United States and democracy, on the other hand, as the forces for good. Our country's long-standing conflict with communism often was described using a similar dichotomy. The job of good is to eliminate the forces of evil, and the Bible offers many examples of support for pursuing evildoers militarily.

But that is not the only word of the Bible. Romans 3:9 reminds us that "all people . . . are under the power of sin." Paul continues by referring to the Psalms when he says: "'No one is good—/not even one./No one has real understanding;/no one is seeking God./All have turned away from God;/all have gone wrong./No one does good,/not even one.'/'Their talk is foul, like the stench from an open grave./Their speech is filled with lies.'/'The poison of a deadly snake drips from their lips.'/'Their mouths are full of cursing and bitterness.'/'They are quick to commit murder./Wherever they go, destruction and misery follow them./They do not know what true peace is'" (Rom. 3:10-17, NLT).

War arises out of humanity's sinful nature and the world's estrangement from God.

Chasing too quickly after the wicked in the name of the righteous is dangerous because we often overlook the sin infecting our own hearts. That oversight leads us not to pursue justice but to nurture our own self-righteousness, which in turn creates injustices of its own.

An alternative to retribution at the other end of the spectrum is the pacifist response. Pacifism is rooted in the New Testament, and of all the possible responses to war, reflects the teachings of Jesus most closely. Jesus proclaimed that he came not to abolish the law but to fulfill it, and in doing so, he often raised the bar of ethical behavior:

> You have heard that the law of Moses says, "Do not murder. If you commit murder, you are subject to judgment." But I say, if you are angry with someone, you are subject to judgment! . . .
> You have heard that the law of Moses says, "If an eye is injured, injure the eye of the person who did it. If a tooth gets knocked out, knock out the tooth of the person who did it." But I say, don't resist an evil person! If you are slapped on the right cheek, turn the other, too. . . . You have heard that the law of Moses says, "Love your neighbor" and hate your enemy. But I say, love your enemies! Pray for those who persecute you! (Matt. 5:21-22, 38-39, 43-44, NLT).

Violence was not an option for Jesus. Even when confronted with the woman who had been caught in adultery, who under the law of Moses deserved to die, Jesus' response was not to undertake the violent sentence of stoning but rather to call attention to human sinfulness. Jesus understood the depth of our sinfulness. He knew that in our heart of hearts we are most concerned with ourselves, that our ultimate focus is always on ourselves. Jesus recognized that human beings possess an unbelievable ability to justify ourselves and rationalize our actions.

In sorting through our response to issues of war, pacifism—or assertive nonviolence—is a significant starting point in our reflection. It is inexcusable to assert that "Christians who willingly and knowingly refuse to engage in a just war do a vicious thing; they fail to show love toward their neighbor as well as toward God" (*Good News*, 29). Pacifism is not vicious but a valid attempt to be true to the example of Jesus. We cannot simply disregard the pacifist perspective as so much sentimentality. We must be willing to admit that our response to war is not merely about meeting three just-war requirements but also about following Jesus.

That being said, what do we do? Do we embrace the military relying on the just war theory and the Old Testament witness, or do we stand with the pacifists who embrace the New Testament ethic of nonviolence? We believe the answer lies somewhere in between. We believe that in the kingdom of God peace and justice exist together; unfortunately, in our sinful world we have difficulty appropriately connecting the two. We err both in overlooking our own sinfulness as we pursue justice and in not taking the depths of human evil in the world seriously as we pursue peace. The sad reality is that until Jesus comes again, we will continue to face circumstances in which unjust power can be met only with power. That reality should never be met with excitement but with lament, because war never arises out of love or virtue, as some may assert in the fervor of their patriotism; rather, war arises out of humanity's sinful nature and the world's estrangement from God. We need to avoid labeling this reality "just," lest our desire for revenge overwhelm our commitment to peace.

This middle way recognizes that the use of force involves what Mark Galli calls "tragic courage," requiring us honestly to accept the responsibility for morally troubling actions. In war lives are taken both deliberately and accidentally; combatants as well as innocents lose their lives. Just-war theory does not eliminate our moral responsibility for these outcomes. When Todd Beamer and several others on United Airlines Flight 93 resisted the hijackers and forced their plane to crash in Pennsylvania, they exhibited tragic courage, shouldering the responsibility of deliberately sacrificing not only their own lives but also the lives of all the others on the plane.

The middle way necessitates that we make commitments to political leadership that is far from pure. We may have great confidence in our country, but the United States is not perfect in its relationships with other nations of the world or even in relationships among its own citizens. History shows all too clearly that national self-interest along with political and economic greed and arrogance often motivate national behavior. It has happened in the past; we must not lull ourselves into thinking it will not happen again.

The middle way requires courage to risk making moral compromises in order to seek justice. That risk requires that we depend all the more on God's grace for our justification, because when we have completed our task, it will be impossible to look back with any sense of pride on the purity of our actions. It is easy to hunt out evil if we think of ourselves as untainted; it takes courage to admit, even as we are seeking to root out international evil, that evil lies within our own hearts. Following the middle path seems to be the only way to honor the demand for justice while at the same time clinging to a commitment to ultimate peace.

War places a huge burden on Christians. Carrying that burden requires humility and a clear recognition that we can never know God's will perfectly at every turn on the political road. We also need to understand the depth of war's sadness and to acknowledge that in our sin-sick world, justice is often impossible without some violence. That acknowledgment prompts us to pray ever more fervently for the coming of Christ, when swords will be hammered into plowshares and spears into pruning hooks, when the wolf will lie down with the lamb and a more perfect world will be shepherded in.

REFLECTING AND RECORDING

Record new insights, questions, disagreements you have with this discussion on war.

Toward which view do you find yourself moving as you respond to questions of war in our time? Do you promote a pacifist approach? a just-war approach?

Imagine having a conversation with Jesus about war. What might you say to each other?

Spend the balance of your time reflecting on the following statements:

"There is a time for everything. . . . a time to love and a time to hate. A time for war and a time for peace" (Eccles. 3:1, 8, NLT).

———⊗⊗⊗———

It is a dangerous thing to chase too quickly after the wicked in the name of righteousness because we often overlook the sin that infects our own hearts.

———⊗⊗⊗———

We err both in overlooking our own sinfulness as we pursue justice, and in not taking the depths of human evil in the world seriously as we pursue peace.

⸰⸰⸰

The middle way is tragic because it requires us to risk making moral compromises in order to seek justice.

⸰⸰⸰

DURING THE DAY

Whenever you see a national or state flag or any other symbol of government, pray for governmental leaders, for their capacity to discern and courage to make the best decisions for justice and the common good.

Seek to engage in conversation a person whose position on war differs from yours.

DAY 7
Killing That Does Not Take Life

> You have heard that it was said to those of ancient times, "You shall not murder"; and "whoever murders shall be liable to judgment." But I say to you that if you are angry with a brother or sister, you will be liable to judgment; and if you insult a brother or sister, you will be liable to the council; and if you say, "You fool," you will be liable to the hell of fire. So when you are offering your gift at the altar, if you remember that your brother or sister has something against you, leave your gift there before the altar and go; first be reconciled to your brother or sister, and then come and offer your gift."—Matthew 5:21-24

This scripture passage is the most heart-searching application of this commandment in the life of the believer. The Sermon on the Mount is Jesus' law for his people, for those who are members of his family in the kingdom. Here Jesus traces murder to its ugly source. Someone has said in response to this passage, "The Savior is interested not only in knocking the gun out of a man's hand but in taking the devil out of his heart."

Three times in this passage Jesus uses the term *brother*. In the presence of God, and when we consider the requirements laid upon us by Christ himself, all are brothers and sisters. The cross of Jesus, where we find forgiveness, not only provides us atonement but demands that we relate to others in the way Jesus has related to us. Since we are forgiven by Jesus, we are called always to forgive others.

Jesus warns, "If you say, 'raca,' you will be liable to the hell of fire" (Matt. 5:22). The word *raca,* translated "fool," is an Aramaic term of contempt. The same principle that forbids us to murder forbids us to treat our fellow human beings contemptuously, refusing to acknowledge their claim to our consideration and respect.

This commandment not only forbids anger but the outgrowth of anger that festers and hardens in our hearts, turning anger into hatred. Paul said, "Do not let the sun go down on your anger" (Eph. 4:26). He knew that anger can boil within us until our hatred for another makes us a murderer even though no blood has been spilled. Anger and hate slay thousands, but crass indifference slays ten thousand. Indifference may be the deadliest sin and the most common among us who call ourselves Christian. In his book *The Surrender and the Singing*, Ray Ashford wrote, "I once watched a man murder a beautiful and intelligent woman. It wasn't, mind you, a crime of passion in which he took her life with a knife or gun in a single explosive moment of blinding rage. It was, rather, a crime absolutely devoid of passion, a murder within the law and over a long period of time, four and a half decades. It was murder by indifference and neglect" (Dunnam, *Perceptions*, 35).

We have all seen murder by indifference and neglect, felt it, and we have to confess, committed it ourselves—by smashing a dream, choking an idea, crushing enthusiasm, putting someone down, implying he or she was less than whole. We need to remember that there is killing that may not take away physical life.

REFLECTING AND RECORDING

Spend a few minutes reflecting on this statement: The Savior is interested not only in knocking the gun out of a man's hand but in taking the devil out of his heart.

Write a prayer confessing how your anger, hatred, bitterness, envy, grudge, or any other "feeling of your heart" damaged another. Examine your feelings now. Are there deep heart feelings from which you need to be released because they have the potential of "killing" another?

Consider whether you are "murdering" neighbors—family, friends, colleagues at work—by indifference or neglect. Name those persons in your heart, pray for them, and pray that the Lord will take away whatever is causing you to be indifferent and give you a heart of compassion.

DURING THE DAY

Think of a person whom you may have neglected or toward whom you've been indifferent. Call or write that person today and begin to restore your relationship.

Group Meeting for Week Six

Leader: This session may generate the most varying opinions and depth of feeling. Ask the group to be understanding of others, not defensive or disrespectful. Plan the time in order that all views will receive consideration.

SHARING TOGETHER

You are approaching the end of this workbook venture. Only two more meetings remain, so your group may want to discuss its future. Would the group like to stay and use other resources (books, tapes, periodicals) corporately? Think about ways to share this workbook study with others.

    As you begin this session, have someone read the paragraph on page 108 beginning, "The commandment not to kill more sharply polarizes . . ."

1. The foundation for the sixth commandment is the fact of humankind's infinite value to the Creator. Spend two or three minutes discussing each of the following statements:

   • Life is sacred because it is a gift of God.

   • Life is sacred because of its God-given purpose.

   • Life is sacred because God has redeemed life.

2. Spend five to eight minutes discussing the claim that murder is wrong because it violates the sanctity of life and usurps God's authority to determine when life will end.

3. Spend four to six minutes responding to the suggestion that there are more sacred things in life than "the sacredness of life." Ask if anyone can share a witness of someone's willingness to sacrifice life for the sake of truth or the faith.

4. Spend ten to twelve minutes discussing capital punishment. Remember, Christians have different opinions on this issue. Be open-minded and receptive to the ideas and feelings of others.

5. Invite persons to share any new insights or questions in considering euthanasia.

6. Does a member of the group have a witness to share about a "good death"—death with dignity or when the withdrawal of life support was involved?

7. Invite someone to share an experience of learning and faith development that resulted from observing someone they knew face death.

8. Is there a person in the group who will share a witness of God's using his or her suffering for good?

9. Ask persons to share any new insights or questions around the issue of abortion.

10. Spend eight to ten minutes sharing the insights, questions, and/or disagreements participants had with the discussion on war.

11. The authors suggested a "middle way" in response to war. Invite a couple of people to respond to this statement: The middle way requires courage to risk making moral compromises in order to seek justice.

12. Spend whatever time you have left discussing "killing that does not take physical life." Ask group members whether they have experienced such killing. Are they guilty of it? Have they observed it happening to another?

PRAYING TOGETHER

Nothing brings people together more than praying together. As we pray for others we come to accept and love them, even though we may disagree with them. Prayer does not dissolve differences but enables us to transcend them, valuing persons as brothers and sisters loved by God.

In this prayer time, experiment with some different ways of praying.

1. Begin by asking the group to name persons they know who are in the military; then ask a volunteer to offer a prayer for these persons.

2. Does the group know anyone who is/has been charged with a crime and is facing trial? anyone presently serving a prison sentence? anyone on death row? Name these persons and ask someone to pray for them.

3. *Leader:* Guide the group in silent or verbal prayer in this way:

   "Let us pray silently for those we know who are pregnant and unmarried and/or wrestling with what to do now."

   "Let us pray aloud or silently for single parents, especially single mothers who are struggling to make it alone."

   "Are there adult persons who are having to make decisions about dying spouses or parents? [Allow time for the participants to speak their names.] Will someone now offer a verbal prayer for these?"

   "Let's spend some time now in silence praying for persons we know who are being killed emotionally, those who are in destructive relationships, dysfunctional families, those who are victims of hatred."

4. Close by praying together the Lord's Prayer and singing a couple of verses of a familiar hymn or a chorus.

Week Seven

Respecting the Person and Property of Others

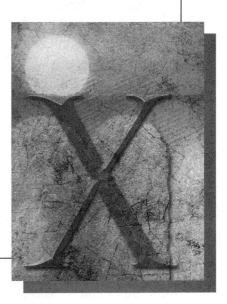

DAY 1

Stealing—Taking What Rightly Belongs to Another

You shall not steal. You shall not bear false witness against your neighbor. You shall not covet your neighbor's house; you shall not covet your neighbor's wife, or male or female slave, or ox, or donkey, or anything that belongs to your neighbor.—Exodus 20:15-17

The sixth, seventh, and eighth commandments are the most direct in expression: You shall not murder; you shall not commit adultery; you shall not steal. The commandment against killing and the commandment against stealing center on reverencing human life and respecting the rights of others. Likewise the tenth commandment: "You shall not covet." This week we will consider commandments eight and ten: "You shall not steal. . . . You shall not covet."

To steal is to take by cunning or force that which rightly belongs to another. Martin Luther said, "If we look at mankind in all its conditions, it is nothing but a vast, wide stable full of great thieves" (Luther, *The Large Catechism*, 40). Calling thievery the most common of all the sins that possess us, he said, "Stealing is a widespread, common vice, but people pay so little attention to it that the matter is entirely out of hand. If all who are thieves, though they are unwilling to admit it, were hanged on the gallows, the world would soon be empty, and there would be a shortage of both hangmen and gallows" (Luther, *The Large Catechism*, 39).

A *Saturday Evening Post* cover illustration by Norman Rockwell depicts a woman buying her Thanksgiving turkey. As the turkey lies on the scales, both the butcher and his customer have a pleased look as if each knows a secret. Norman Rockwell lets us in on the joke by showing us their hands. The butcher is pushing down on the scales with a big fat thumb. The woman is pushing up on them with a dainty forefinger. Neither is aware of what the other is doing.

Cecil Meyers says of that painting, "Both the butcher and the lovely lady would resent being called thieves. The little lady would never rob a bank or steal a car. The butcher would be indignant if anyone accused him of stealing; and if a customer gave him a bad check, he would call the police. But neither saw anything wrong with a little deception that would make a few cents for one or save a few cents for the other" (Meyers, *Thunder on the Mountain*, 119–20).

Rockwell illustrates the human tendency to manipulate life to our advantage. At the heart of it, that's what this prohibition against stealing is all about. Luther's startling claim about widespread thievery begins to be credible when we recognize stealing in the failure to pay wages that are due, cheating on income tax returns, fraud in buying or selling, paying money for promotions or positions, taking advantage of someone up against a wall, withholding from others whatever they have a right to expect from us, refusing to pay a debt. Stealing can be either active or passive—not just taking from others what is theirs but withholding from others what we ought to give.

In his instruction to the church at Ephesus, Paul says, "Thieves must give up stealing; rather let them labor and work honestly with their own hands, so as to have something to share with the needy" (Eph. 4:28). There are three clear demands in that one sentence. (1) We must not steal. (2) We are to engage in honest labor. (3) We are to labor and be productive in order that we might "have something to share with the needy."

Paul's admonition to the Ephesians should cause us to sit up and pay attention. If Paul had a favorite church, it was this church in Ephesus, a congregation that provided him the greatest joy. To "the saints in Ephesus, the faithful in Christ Jesus" he wrote, "He who has been stealing must steal no longer" (Eph. 1:1; 4:28, NIV). What? Thieves in church! The truth is, most of us are in congregations where more people violate the commandments against stealing and lying than any others. Unfortunately, deceit is a common malady.

REFLECTING AND RECORDING

Spend a few minutes thinking about the congregation of which you are a part. In what ways are we right in saying that "most of us are in congregations where more people violate the commandments against stealing and lying than any others"?

Because the church is essential as the supportive community for our living the commandments, continue your reflection on the congregation of which you are a part. How do the teaching and preaching reflect the demands of the Ten Commandments and the gospel?

Make a list of groups or programs that provide guidance, support, and inspiration for people to live the commandments in the marketplace.

How can your congregation become a place of hospitality—welcoming people, accepting diversity, seeking to understand lifestyles and life experiences?

Consider whether your congregation proclaims righteousness, holiness, and justice without condemning, receiving persons in grace where they are but offering the possibility that they will not remain as they are.

DURING THE DAY

Note the instances of passive and active stealing that you observe today.

DAY 2
A Sin Against God and Against Humankind

> When you make your neighbor a loan of any kind, you shall not go into the house to take the pledge. You shall wait outside, while the person to whom you are making the loan brings the pledge out to you. If the person is poor, you shall not sleep in the garment given you as the pledge. You shall give the pledge back by sunset, so that your neighbor may sleep in the cloak and bless you; and it will be to your credit before the LORD your God. You shall not withhold the wages of poor and needy laborers, whether other Israelites or aliens who reside in your land in one of your towns. You shall pay them their wages daily before sunset, because they are poor and their livelihood depends on them; otherwise they might cry to the LORD against you, and you would incur guilt.—Deuteronomy 24:10-15

Throughout the years, Jewish commentators on this commandment have referred to "the sanctity of property." Property was, for most Hebrews, their only means of livelihood. If someone stole their flocks or drove away their cattle, they could not survive. Nomads for most of their national history, the Hebrews had no bank where they could make a deposit, no insurance companies to cover their losses. Theft could destroy them or impoverish them forever.

Apart from this commandment, scripture, especially the Old Testament, says a lot about property. The Bible makes clear that stealing is a sin against God because it betrays our trust in God, and it is a sin against humankind because it denies love and concern for others. Strictly speaking, theft is taking or keeping what is not ours, yet it is more. While the Bible defends the right to own property, it pronounces judgment upon those who injure others in the pursuit of property.

> Thus says the LORD:/For three transgressions of Judah,/and for four, I will not revoke the punishment;/because they have rejected the law of the LORD,/and have not kept his statutes,/but they have been led astray by the same lies/after which their ancestors walked./So I will send a fire on Judah,/and it shall devour the strongholds of Jerusalem.
>
> Thus says the LORD:/For three transgressions of Israel,/and for four, I will not revoke the punishment;/because they sell the righteous for silver,/and the needy for a pair of sandals—/they

who trample the head of the poor into the dust of the earth,/and push the afflicted out of the way;/father and son go in to the same girl,/so that my holy name is profaned (Amos 2:4-7).

Ours is a society "on the take." Officers of large corporate organizations preside in posh board rooms while manipulating the stock market. "Cost overrides" steal millions of tax dollars. There is often a fine distinction between criminal and legal activity, as evidenced by the biggest bankruptcy in American history at Enron, the world's largest energy company. The words of the prophet Amos apply to those who filled their coffers with wealth by selling their stock while denying their employees the right to sell theirs: "They . . . trample the head of the poor into the dust of the earth" (Amos 2:7).

REFLECTING AND RECORDING

Reflect on this statement: Stealing is a sin against God because it betrays our trust in God.

—— ❦ ——

Consider this statement: Stealing is a sin against humankind because it denies love and concern for others.

—— ❦ ——

Recall and make notes about the a recent case of persons being injured by others' pursuit of property and wealth.

Note any situation you know in which people are acting legally but not morally in their treatment of others.

Identify situations in your community where the church and other institutions are not actively working to make life more livable for vulnerable people. Make some notes.

DURING THE DAY

Continue today to note the instances of passive and active stealing that you observe.

DAY 3
Stealing—Active and Passive

*I*n one of the most familiar stories in scripture, the parable of the good Samaritan (Luke 10:30-37), two kinds of robbery took place. The aggressive thieves violently stripped the person of his raiment, wounded him, took what he had, and left him half-dead by the wayside. They totally disregarded the rights of their victim. But as the poor man was bleeding on the wayside, a priest came along, then a Levite. Neither stopped. They may have made note of, but they didn't give attention to, this suffering man. No doubt they were decent, law-abiding persons; we know they were religious. Their thievery was passive. They failed to do what they could for a wounded and dying man. Our stealing from others may be as real as active theft if we fail to provide what we could to make a great difference in their lives.

A young man whose son had been killed in an automobile accident poured out his grief—almost overcome by it but with confidence and joy at the same time. Despite his obvious pain, his tear-filled eyes sparkled as he shared the fact that many of his young son's organs, including the boy's eyes and heart, had been used by doctors to save lives and serve the needs of others. What a contrast between this man and the priest and Levite who passed by on the other side.

Perhaps our most blatant act of thievery is withholding care and concern from those around us. Karl Menninger, the eminent psychiatrist, tells us that in our early years we will die if we do not *receive* love. In our later years, he continues, we will wither up and die if we do not *give* love.

REFLECTING AND RECORDING

Spend time reflecting on this claim: Perhaps our most blatant act of thievery is withholding care and concern from those around us. Are you guilty? Is the Christian community of which you are a part guilty? In what ways?

In *Laws of Christian Living*, Perry McDonald and William Odell contend that while Jesus taught the same spiritual vision about materialism contained in the Old Testament, he added three major teachings: *reform, conversion,* and *restitution.* Reflect on two of these.

Conversion

Jesus highlighted the conversion message by challenging all to place their priorities carefully: "No one can serve two masters. He will either hate one and love the other or be attentive to one and despise the other. You cannot give yourself to God and money" (Matt. 6:24). He reminded his listeners that "where your treasure is, there your heart is also" (Matt. 6:21).

The message is vividly illustrated in the story about the rich young man. While speaking to the rich man, Jesus told him that obedience to the commandments would provide him with a share in everlasting life. The man replied that he had kept the commandments, so Jesus told him to sell all and give to the poor. That was more than the rich man could swallow. Jesus then lamented about how hard it was for the rich to enter the kingdom of God. The young man refused to give up his possessions because he placed his personal security in them rather than in God. Material possessions can give an illusion of security. As possessions and wealth increase, they threaten a tighter hold on the human heart (Luke 18:18-25) (McDonald and Odell, *Laws of Christian Living*, 149).

What is the message here for you?

⸺ ❈ ⸺

Restitution

In no place in Scripture does Jesus speak about restitution, the practice of returning or making amends for what was stolen. But Jesus did praise the action of Zacchaeus, the tax collector who had climbed a tree to listen to him. Zacchaeus was so honored when Jesus told him that he wanted to stay at his house, that the tax collector decided to make amends for overtaxing. He told Jesus: "If I have defrauded anyone in the least, I pay him back fourfold" (Luke 19:8). Perhaps Zacchaeus was simply following what he knew God wanted, stated as it was in Exodus: "When a man steals an ox or a sheep and slaughters or sells it, he shall restore five oxen for the one ox, and four sheep for the one sheep" (Exod. 21:37). Added to his action of offering restitution, Zacchaeus also professed that "I give half my belongings, Lord, to the poor" (Luke 19:8). To Jesus, Zacchaeus's sharing of his property and his great desire to make restitution for anything which he stole was evidence that he was a true believer (*Laws of Christian Living*, 150).

What is the message here for you? Is there someone to whom you need to make restitution?

⸺ ❈ ⸺

DURING THE DAY

Register in your mind persons or groups of people in your community who are suffering because care and concern are being withheld from them. At least three times today, pray for them. In your praying, seek guidance for the kind of action you and others might take to express care and concern.

DAY 4
Depriving Another Is Stealing

On Day 2 of this week we considered the important place of property in the life of the Hebrew people. For the Hebrews, property was a gift of God—God giving them a stake in creation. So connected was the property with the person that not even a king had the right to appropriate one of his subjects' properties. Here is such a story in 1 Kings:

> Naboth the Jezreelite had a vineyard in Jezreel, beside the palace of King Ahab of Samaria. And Ahab said to Naboth, "Give me your vineyard, so that I may have it for a vegetable garden, because it is near my house; I will give you a better vineyard for it; or, if it seems good to you, I will give you its value in money." But Naboth said to Ahab, "The LORD forbid that I should give you my ancestral inheritance." Ahab went home resentful and sullen because of what Naboth the Jezreelite had said to him; for he had said, "I will not give you my ancestral inheritance." He lay down on his bed, turned away his face, and would not eat (1 Kings 21:1-4).

Aware of the law forbidding him to confiscate or force a purchase of a subject's land, Ahab would not press his claim further. But Ahab's wife, Jezebel, a foreign princess who owed no loyalty to the law of Israel, engineered a false charge against Naboth, then called witnesses and had him stoned to death, so that Ahab could take possession of the vineyard. Then Elijah the prophet appeared on the scene.

> Then the word of the LORD came to Elijah the Tishbite, saying: Go down to meet King Ahab of Israel, who rules in Samaria; he is now in the vineyard of Naboth, where he has gone to take possession. You shall say to him, "Thus says the LORD: Have you killed, and also taken possession?" You shall say to him, "Thus says the LORD: In the place where dogs licked up the blood of Naboth, dogs will also lick up your blood" (1 Kings 21:17-19).

Note how murder and theft are associated in the prophet's mind; stealing is no casual thing. The righteousness of God undergirds both commandments. Depriving others of that which gives meaning to their existence deprives them of their dignity as well. Slavery and later Jim Crow laws, in law and practice, robbed African Americans of their dignity, denying them the right to vote, forcibly segregating them in neighborhoods and schools, and robbing them of justice. In the United States women have been denied rights that for men were never questioned; along with African Americans, they continue to face bias even to this day.

Far less dramatic but common is the damage done to a person's reputation when we impugn his or her character with outright lies, innuendo, or silence rather than defense of the individual. We also violate this commandment when we use our advantage over another person for our gain or satisfaction. Deuteronomy 24 warns against taking advantage of a hired man who is poor and needy, "whether he is a brother Israelite or an alien living in one of your towns. Pay him his wages each day before sunset, because he is poor and is counting on it" (vv. 14-15, NIV). We steal from others when we use our economic or other advantage to control them and when we fail to give them their due. In the witness of scripture, those who have must pay attention to and be generous toward those who have not (Deut. 24:19-22).

Most everyone using this workbook is rich compared to the population of the world. All of us have that which we can share; therefore, all of us should pay attention to James's stern warning:

> Come now, you rich people, weep and wail for the miseries that are coming to you. Your riches have rotted, and your clothes are moth-eaten. Your gold and silver have rusted, and their rust will be evidence against you, and it will eat your flesh like fire. You have laid up treasure for the last days. Listen! The wages of the laborers who mowed your fields, which you kept back by fraud, cry out, and the cries of the harvesters have reached the ears of the Lord of hosts. You have lived on the earth in luxury and in pleasure; you have fattened your hearts in a day of slaughter. You have condemned and murdered the righteous one, who does not resist you (James 5:1-6).

Most of us wouldn't think of ourselves as "wealthy." Addressing the graduating medical school class of McGill University a few generations ago, Rudyard Kipling said, "You'll go from here, and very likely you'll make a lot of money. One day you'll meet someone for whom that means very little. Then you will know how poor you are" (quoted in *Leadership*, vol 16, no. 4, 21).

REFLECTING AND RECORDING

Stealing is a sin against God because it betrays our trust in God. Our attitude toward wealth and material things also betrays that trust. Jesus told a consoling story of God's care for the lilies, the birds, the grass of the field, and concluded, "If God so clothes the grass of the field, which is alive today and tomorrow is thrown into the oven, how much more will he clothe you—you of little faith! And do not keep striving for what you are to eat and what you are to drink, and do not keep worrying. For it is the nations of the world that strive after all these things, and your Father knows that you need them" (Luke 12:28-30).

Spend some time reflecting on what in your life betrays your trust in God, paying special attention to your attitude toward wealth and material things.

———— ✎ ————

Take a hard look at your community. Note people who are being deprived of their dignity and exploited economically. Are there conversations going on about these issues? Is your congregation involved in a redemptive way? What might you do about such situations?

DURING THE DAY

Continue to register in your mind persons or groups of people in your community who are suffering because care and concern are being withheld from them. At least three times today, pray for them, seeking guidance for the kind of action you and others might take to express care and concern.

DAY 5
To Desire Earnestly

> You shall not covet your neighbor's house; you shall not covet your neighbor's wife, or male or female slave, or ox, or donkey, or anything that belongs to your neighbor.—Exodus 20:17

*T*his commandment warns against desiring, seeking, and getting more than we need or can possibly use. In the ancient day, coveting was the first stage of actual stealing. The prophet Micah explained the flow of coveting into stealing: "Alas for those who devise wickedness/and evil deeds on their beds!/When the morning dawns, they perform it,/because it is in their power./They covet fields, and seize them;/houses, and take them away;/they oppress householder and house,/people and their inheritance" (Mic. 2:1-2).

One meaning of the word *covet* is "to desire earnestly." Another meaning is "delight." There is a link between the two. We normally desire what is delightful. Scripture calls for that kind of desiring on our part in our relation to God and the kingdom. In fact Jesus' summary of the commandments is a call to desire earnestly: "You shall love the Lord your God with all your heart, and with all your soul, and with all your strength and with all your mind" (Luke 10:27). "Make this the ultimate desire of your heart," Jesus said (AP). "Seek ye first the kingdom of God, and [God's] righteousness; and all these things shall be added unto you" (Matt. 6:33, KJV).

As Stuart Briscoe has reminded us,

> the command does not imply that we should have no desires and delight in nothing. God initially gave us the desires and filled the world with delightful things for us to enjoy. Having given them, however, [God] warns us, "Now don't desire delightful things wrongly." That statement clearly confronts us with the problems of identifying those wrong desires and admitting to ourselves how we have mishandled delightful things. We need to find the right balance, because along with giving us the desires and delightful things, God has also denied us certain things. If we ignore what God has set off limits, simply allowing our desires to go unfettered, we find ourselves deep in covetousness (Briscoe, *The Ten Commandments*, 172).

The Hebrew word for desire, *hamad*, is a neutral word, implying nothing good or bad. Paul reminded us that we ought to "earnestly desire the best gifts" (1 Cor. 12:31, NKJV). But desire that causes us to want what belongs to another or to go after something to which we have no right is covetousness. What we covet tells the story of our lives, because what we will give our devotion and energy to we earnestly desire. All the other commandments that relate to the relationship among human beings focus on outward, visible actions, but this commandment focuses on inner motives. We find it easier to talk about the others because we can identify and verify actions, while attitudes may remain hidden. Actually human covetousness is assumed in many of the other commandments. Covetousness often underlies our violation of the law. The Hebrew word for *covet* includes "lust," which we considered when we talked about adultery. In this context Jesus provided a perspective on covetousness: "You have heard that it was said, 'Do not commit adultery.' But I tell you that anyone who looks at a woman lustfully has already committed adultery with her in his heart'" (Matt. 5:27, NIV).

Most of us are guilty of coveting that reflects desire for what others possess and our almost insatiable desire for more. One commentator has remarked aptly that not only is coveting a sin, but it's stupid. We're convinced we have a cosmic right to an equal share of life's good things, a fallacious idea that plays havoc in our lives. There is no equality in talents, abilities, opportunities, or even in being in the right place at the right time. When we feel we have a right to an equal share of what "everybody else" has, a good antidote is to consider how much we'd have if we averaged out shares with the world's two billion starving people.

REFLECTING AND RECORDING

List three things that you earnestly desire:

1.

2.

3.

How do these three things represent healthy or destructive coveting? Are there ways you may be desiring these "delightful things" wrongly?

———— ✺ ————

How do the three things you desire fit with Paul's admonition to "covet earnestly the best gifts"?

———— ✺ ————

Test yourself with these questions:

• Do I feel entitled to an equal share of the good things of life?

———— ✺ ————

• What are the things others have that I desire and feel I deserve?

———— ✺ ————

• How insatiable is my desire for more?

• Can I be happy with what I have and where I am in life?

DURING THE DAY

Today and throughout this week, measure any desire that comes to you against this word of Jesus: "But strive first for the kingdom of God and [God's] righteousness, and all these things will be given to you as well" (Matt. 6:33).

DAY 6
You Shall Not Covet

"Neither shall you covet your neighbor's wife" (Deut. 5:21). This last commandment has probably received the least attention of all the commandments. In all our churches and in the public arena, we hear far more about stealing, adultery, killing, lying. John C. Maxwell has confessed that he used to consider this "the weak sister" of the commandments. "It has occurred to me," he said, "that whoever approved the final order of these commandments didn't have much of a sense of suspense or climax. He put all of those dramatic, intriguing sins like stealing, adultery, and murder first. Then he ended with coveting. It would have seemed more logical to begin with the bland, throw-away sin like coveting, and then work up to the big stuff" (Maxwell, in *The Communicator's Commentary*, vol. 5, 267).

Though we may not covet our neighbor's spouse, servants, ox, or donkey, what about position, money, opportunity? Don't we look at others, compare ourselves to them, and conclude that we have come out on the short end? We drive ourselves to depression, thinking that we deserve more and dreaming of how happy we would be if we were in someone else's situation. All these feelings indicate we have fallen into the subtle, seductive hands of covetousness. So a bit of honest reflection is in order.

When did you last have the thought that some other person got the breaks while you did not?

Have you thought recently that you were deprived of some opportunity?

Have you had the notion that your friends are where they are because they had far more opportunities than you did?

———— ∞ ————

When do you most often find yourself thinking about the injustice of the system?

———— ∞ ————

When our desires are disordered and excessive, we become covetous. *Concupiscence* is a classical Christian word that we normally associate with sensuality, uncontrolled passion, especially sexual passion. But the word applies to the total range of our desires because it suggests intensity—inordinate, unchecked, excessive. When such desire turns away from God or is not disciplined by our relationship with God, everything else becomes distorted.

The rising tide of consumerism perhaps most vividly expresses covetousness as the sin of our society. A materialistic civilization condemns its citizens to slavery to things, economic systems, production. Preoccupied with acquiring more and more stuff, we become insensitive to the needs of others, indifferent to the poverty in the world. The United States represents only 6 percent of the earth's population, yet we consume 33 to 40 percent of the planet's food, energy, and other resources.

We can do something about this imbalance by individually asking ourselves: How many things do I need to have a happy and full life? Is the way I am living what life is all about? Have I unwittingly begun to serve material things rather than God? Then we can also join with others who take a critical look at the values inherent in our culture, and become involved in seeking to make those values more applicable to all people—so that justice and mercy will prevail.

From the fountain of covetousness flows poison water. If we break this commandment—if we are covetous—the chances are we will violate other commandments as well. Paul even connected covetousness with idolatry: "Put to death, therefore, whatever belongs to your earthly nature: sexual immorality, impurity, lust, evil desires and greed, which is idolatry" (Col. 3:5, NIV).

REFLECTING AND RECORDING

In the teaching of the New Testament, the eighth and tenth commandments are reduced to a few simple truths. Reflect on those in turn:

God loves us, and we should trust God's providence.

———— ∞ ————

If we love God and seek God's reign over us, we will lack nothing we really need.

———— ∞ ————

Coveting and stealing not only are *not needed* for success and happiness in life; they lead to present and future unhappiness.

———— ∞ ————

DURING THE DAY

Pay attention to all the advertisements you see and hear today—in newspapers, on billboards, on TV and radio. How are they appealing to you and leading you to the sin of covetousness?

Continue confronting any desire that comes to you today with this word of Jesus, "But strive first for the kingdom of God and [God's] righteousness, and all these things will be give to you as well" (Matt. 6:33).

DAY 7
The Remedy for Covetousness

Vernard Eller provides a good perspective on the power of covetousness to cause further sin: "A person who wants something so bad he can taste it hardly is free to taste all the good and wonderful things that are already available" (Eller, **MAD** *Morality*, 77). This comment reminds me of a story about William Randolph Hearst, the famous newspaper owner and multi-millionaire. Hearst once saw the print of a famous painting and decided he wanted the original. He hired a detective to find it. Several months and several thousand dollars later, the detective returned with good news and bad news. The good news was he had found the painting. The bad news was he had found it in one of Mr. Hearst's own warehouses. Hearst already owned it!

Eller also describes a covetous person as being in a jail built with the bars of unrealistic and unhealthy desires. On the other hand, one of the freest persons the world has ever seen was the apostle Paul, who, while sitting in a literal jail, nevertheless could write, 'I have learned, in whatever state I am, to be content'" (Eller, **MAD** *Morality*, 77).

Paul was concerned about people. He declared on one occasion that he had become all things to all people, in order that he might be an effective Christian witness to them (1 Cor. 9:22). So he wasn't content with persons as they were, nor with himself as he was. He confessed, "I do not consider that I have made it my own; but this one thing I do: forgetting what lies behind and straining forward to what lies ahead, I press on toward the goal for the prize of the heavenly call of God in Christ Jesus" (Phil. 3:13-14). Contented simply with his relationship to Christ and the direction in which his life was moving, he claimed that though he possessed nothing, he possessed everything.

Contentment and meaning do not come from what we have but from the satisfaction in making a contribution through our relationships with others and especially through our relationship with the Lord. Yet it is very hard to resist the spirit of our age, which dictates consuming more and more. The Gospels of Matthew, Mark, and Luke tell a story that challenges us at this point. Here is the Lukan version:

A certain ruler asked him, "Good Teacher, what must I do to inherit eternal life?" Jesus said to him, "Why do you call me good? No one is good but God alone. You know the commandments:

'You shall not commit adultery; You shall not murder; You shall not steal; You shall not bear false witness; Honor your father and mother.'" He replied, "I have kept all these since my youth." When Jesus heard this, he said to him, "There is still one thing lacking. Sell all that you own and distribute the money to the poor, and you will have treasure in heaven; then come, follow me." But when he heard this, he became sad; for he was very rich (Luke 18:18-23).

Where our treasure is, there our hearts are going to be. The answer to covetousness is to set our minds and hearts on Jesus Christ—to seek first his kingdom, confident that all else needed for joy and meaning will be ours.

Happiness and joy are an inside job, coming from the inner citadel of freedom that belongs to all of us, the inner place where we make our choices. If we lose touch with that center, we usually end up coveting that which can never make us happy, failing to realize that what matters most is not what becomes of us but what we become; we determine that. G. K. Chesterton suggested that there are at least two ways to be rich. One is to have a lot of possessions; the other is to have few needs. To win the battle over coveting requires putting our needs in the proper perspective and diminishing our wants to a manageable level.

REFLECTING AND RECORDING

The following questions will enable you to make an examination of the extent to which the sin of covetousness reigns in your life. Spend time with each question.

Have I coveted anything that belongs to someone else?

When have I cheated for my own material gain or interest?

How do I respect the property and possessions of others, including the property of institutions?

When have I been deeply envious of the possessions, accomplishments, or personal gifts of others?

Do I spend so much money on my desires that I do not share as much as I could with others? Why?

To what degree am I seduced by the rising tide of consumerism?

In what ways do I depend upon my material possessions to give me a sense of security?

How do I live in the confidence that God will provide for all my needs and those of my family?

Spend the balance of the time you have reflecting on this claim: To win the battle over coveting requires putting our needs in the proper perspective and diminishing our wants to a responsible level.

DURING THE DAY

Continue measuring any desire that comes to you against this word of Jesus: "Seek first the kingdom of God and His righteousness, and all these things shall be added to you" (Matt. 6:33, NKJV).

Group Meeting for Week Seven

Leader: You will need a chalkboard or newsprint for this session.

INTRODUCTION

Last week you may have discussed whether your group wants to continue meeting. If so, here are some possibilities to consider.

1. Select two or three weeks of this workbook that were especially difficult or meaningful. Repeat those weeks in more depth to extend your time together.

2. Decide to continue meeting as a group, using another resource. Appoint two or three members to bring resource suggestions to the group next week.

   If this workbook style is meaningful, there are several others in the series, which you'll find listed in the front of this volume.

3. One or two persons may decide to recruit and lead another group through this workbook. Many people are looking for a small-group experience, and this is a way to respond to their need.

SHARING TOGETHER

1. You have only one more group meeting. Invite a couple of volunteers to share what this experience has meant to them thus far.

2. Spend eight to ten minutes discussing the ministry of your church in relation to the Ten Commandments. Do the teaching and preaching reflect the demands of the Ten Commandments? Are there programs and support for people to live the commandments in the marketplace? Education? Ministry to persons with gambling addiction? Counseling for those faced with unwanted pregnancies? Ministry for expectant single mothers? Is your congregation a place of hospitality, welcoming people, accepting diversity, seeking to understand lifestyles and life experiences?

3. Look at your community. How is the commandment against stealing being broken in ways other than obvious "stealing," such as armed robbery? Spend four to six minutes talking about this distinction and examples.

4. Invite two or three persons to respond to the statement: Perhaps our most blatant act of thievery is withholding care and concern from those around us.

5. Spend four to six minutes discussing stealing as depriving others of that which gives meaning to their existence.

6. Take another look at your community. Are some persons taking economic advantage of others? Are vulnerable people not receiving protection from those who prey upon them? Could your church do anything about this situation?

7. Ask two people to describe, without naming, the most covetous person they know and the "fallout" of that person's way of living.

8. Ask the group to name what they "covet" most—things they don't have or do have but want more of. These desires may be tangible (material) or intangible (status, publicity, power). As items are named, list them on a chalkboard or newsprint.

   Now look at the list. Put a check (✓) beside those that result primarily from the influence of today's consumer culture. Put an asterisk (★) beside those that stem from our human nature.

   Spend a few minutes talking about how items in both categories are sin against others and/or sin against God. What would happen to you if you were granted your desires? What kind of persons would you become?

9. Ask the group to spend six to eight minutes discussing the suggestion that "we convince ourselves that we have a cosmic right to an equal share of the good things of life."

10. Spend the balance of your time sharing responses to these two statements: (1) There are two ways to be rich: One is to have a lot of possessions; the other is to have few needs. (2) To win the battle over coveting is to put our needs in the proper perspective and diminish our wants to a responsible level.

PRAYING TOGETHER

Invite persons to take turns offering prayer in the following categories:
- a prayer confessing our sin of withholding care and concern for those around us
- a prayer confessing the sin of the church in not paying attention to persons over whom others are taking economic advantage
- a prayer confessing our sin of coveting
- a prayer of intercession for the poor of our community and for groups within the community that are ministering to the poor

Close your prayer time by inviting someone to read the story of the good Samaritan in Luke 10:30-37.

Week Eight

Nothing but the Truth

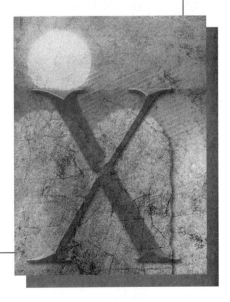

DAY 1
You Shall Not Bear False Witness

*M*ost of us have heard the old saying "Sticks and stones may break my bones, but words will never hurt me." Not true! Words do hurt. In fact, they can be deadly.

The commandment "You shall not bear false witness against your neighbor" (Exod. 20:16) originated in the court where witnesses were under oath to tell the truth. However, it is applied broadly as a prohibition against untruthfulness of any kind. Over and over again scripture speaks of the destructive power of the tongue. The psalmist was overwhelmed by the onslaught of his enemies, but his bitterest experience was the false and malicious witness that rose up against him: "Do not turn me over to the desire of my foes,/for false witnesses rise up against me,/breathing out violence" (Ps. 27:12, NIV). "Ruthless witnesses come forward;/they question me on things I know nothing about./They repay me evil for good/and leave my soul forlorn" (Ps. 35:11-12, NIV).

The book of Proverbs identifies as one of the seven things that the Lord hates "a false witness who pours out lies" (6:19, NIV). Repeatedly the proverbs condemn this sin: "Whoever speaks the truth gives honest evidence,/but a false witness speaks deceitfully" (12:17). "A faithful witness does not lie,/but a false witness breathes out lies" (14:5). "Like a war club, a sword, or a sharp arrow/is one who bears false witness against a neighbor" (25:18). "A worthless witness mocks at justice,/and the mouth of the wicked devours iniquity" (19:28). "Do not be a witness against your neighbor without cause,/and do not deceive with your lips" (24:28). "A truthful witness saves lives,/but one who utters lies is a betrayer" (14:25). Also, it is clear from Proverbs that the false witness will be judged by the Lord: "A false witness will not go unpunished, and a liar will not escape" (19:5). "A false witness will perish" (21:28).

The prophets vehemently denounced false witness, moving beyond the narrow sense of false witness as it was understood in the time of Moses. Hosea chastised the Israelites for their idolatry, accusing them of having "eaten the fruit of lies" (10:13). Amos warned the Israelites that Judea and Jerusalem would be devastated because "they have been led astray by the same lies after which their ancestors walked" (2:4). Isaiah chastised the Israelites: "For your hands are defiled with blood,/and your fingers with iniquity;/your lips have spoken lies,/your tongue mutters wickedness" (59:3). Jeremiah was saddened and grieved over the plight of the Israelites because they "make ready their tongue like a bow, to shoot lies" (9:3, NIV). The prophets identified and grieved to the Israelites about the big lie—the lie that denied Yahweh and his power and authority over the Israelites. Centuries later, the evangelist John asked the question "Who is the liar but the one who denies that Jesus is the Christ?'" (1 John 2:22).

Jesus himself dealt with false witnesses in no uncertain terms: "For out of the heart come evil intentions, murder, adultery, fornication, theft, false testimony, slander. These are what defile a person" (Matt. 15:19-20). He confronted the Pharisees with their hypocrisy: "I tell you, on the day of judgment you will have to give an account for every careless word you utter" (Matt. 12:36). Using vivid imagery to describe the Pharisees' daily distortions of the truth, he said they were frauds, for they were "like whitewashed tombs, which on the outside look beautiful, but inside they are full of the bones of the dead and of all kinds of filth" (Matt. 23:27). He called them hypocrites (Matt. 23:27) and vipers because they devoured the savings of widows (Mark 12:40).

A dramatic example of the destructiveness of false witness is Jesus' death sentence handed down on the basis of the Sanhedrin's efforts to obtain false witnesses against Jesus (Matt. 26:59). The high priest, Caiaphas, finally resorted to trumping up a charge of blasphemy. The same fate befell Stephen, who was martyred because of false witnesses.

Jesus was concerned primarily with our being false with God. He reserved his harshest judgment for the Pharisees whose hypocrisy twisted and distorted the truth given to them by God. Their hypocrisy was a slap in the face to God. New Testament writers made it clear: "The man who claims, 'I have known him,' without keeping his commandments is a liar . . ." (1 John 2:4). "If we say that we have fellowship with him while we are walking in darkness, we lie . . ." (1 John 1:6).

REFLECTING AND RECORDING

List five ways we may bear false witness:

1.

2.

3.

4.

5.

Put a check (✓) by those of which you have been guilty in your lifetime.

Look at the past two or three months of your life. When have you been guilty of any of these expressions of bearing false witness? How have you confessed to the Lord? Have you acknowledged your false witness to the person against whom you bore it and asked forgiveness?

Spend a few minutes reflecting on this commandment's relevance to living day in and day out.

DURING THE DAY

Listen carefully to others; pay attention to TV and newspaper stories, advertisements, the way you relate to others and they to you. Identify any false witnessing that is taking place.

DAY 2
Lying to Others

So also the tongue is a small member, yet it boasts of great exploits. How great a forest is set ablaze by a small fire! And the tongue is a fire. The tongue is placed among our members as a world of iniquity; it stains the whole body, sets on fire the cycle of nature, and is itself set on fire by hell. For every species of beast and bird, of reptile and sea creature, can be tamed and has been tamed by the human species, but no one can tame the tongue—a restless evil, full of deadly poison.—James 3:5-8

A wise old proverb says, "Sin has a great many tools, but a lie is the handle that fits them all." A malicious lie, idle gossip, a half-truth, insincere flattery, remaining silent, even a raised eyebrow or shrugged shoulders can bear false witness, hurting and even destroying another person.

Stuart Briscoe identifies four ways in which people tend to lie to their neighbors. The first is the *destructive lie,* born of malicious intent. Because we want to do harm, we do not tell the truth; in fact, we deliberately suggest erroneous information. Sometimes when we are hurt, malice grows in our hearts to a point where we want to destroy someone or put a roadblock in the person's way. We find a biblical example of destructive lying in the efforts of Potiphar's wife to seduce Joseph, who had been sold into slavery in Egypt. When Joseph resisted and ran away so quickly that he left his cloak in her hand, she used the cloak to support her claim that he had assaulted her (Gen. 39). This false accusation put Joseph in jail for a long season.

We use the *defensive lie* to protect ourselves when we are caught and afraid. It is the kind of lie Peter told when he was in the courtyard of the high priest's house, where Jesus was being held. Some persons recognized Peter and accused him three times of being with Jesus, and three times Peter denied it. Scripture says that he broke into oaths and curses, calling on God to witness that he was not one of Christ's disciples.

The *defective lie* is the lie of carelessness, boastfulness, or silence. It is not intentional and may even be a casual exercise. Because we don't like a particular person, we may be quite happy to pass on an unsavory story about him or her. Or, because we need affirmation, we build ourselves up by exaggerating, by stretching the truth to make ourselves look good.

The *half-truth* is not a lie; nor is it the truth. Jesus must have had this kind of lying in mind when he said, "Let your word be 'Yes, Yes' or 'No, No'" (Matt. 5:37). We should strive to be absolutely clear that we are communicating and responding honestly.

REFLECTING AND RECORDING

Often a doctor examines a patient's tongue. How examining the tongue aids a doctor's diagnosis is a mystery to us! But we need to let the Lord Jesus see our tongues. Spend time looking at your own tongue—and allowing Jesus to look at it. In the past week, when have you spoken an unkind word? How unkind was that unkind word?

—— ✺ ——

In the past three or four weeks, when have you added to conversation about someone that did not build that person up?

—— ✺ ——

In the past few weeks, when have you failed to speak up on behalf of a person who was being criticized or defamed falsely?

—— ✺ ——

In the past few weeks, when has someone you know needed comfort that your words could provide—either verbal or written—and you've not yet shared those words?

—— ✺ ——

Recall a time in the past few weeks when you have failed to speak up on an issue that needed your witness in your town, city, or state.

—— ✺ ——

DURING THE DAY

As you move through this day, seek to identify any of these kinds of lying described by Stuart Briscoe as you listen to and talk with people:

- the destructive lie born of malicious intent and made up of entirely erroneous content
- the defensive lie told to get ourselves out of a situation
- the defective lie of carelessness, boastfulness, silence
- the half-truth—neither a lie nor the truth

DAY 3
Hypocrisy

*H*ow often do we see persons pretending to be either better or worse than they really are? How often do we fall into that snare ourselves? The sin of hypocrisy aroused the indignation of Jesus perhaps more than any other. He minced no words and held back no passion when he addressed the issue.

> But woe to you, scribes and Pharisees, hypocrites! For you lock people out of the kingdom of heaven. For you do not go in yourselves, and when others are going in, you stop them. . . . Woe to you, scribes and Pharisees, hypocrites! For you tithe mint, dill, and cummin, and have neglected the weightier matters of the law: justice and mercy and faith. It is these you ought to have practiced without neglecting the others. You blind guides! You strain out a gnat but swallow a camel! (Matt. 23:13-14, 23-24).

It is dishonest to misrepresent one's own character. The Greek word *hypocrite* originally referred to one who wore a mask in Greek dramas. The basic idea is that of matching our true self with our pretended self, or, vice versa, matching our pretended self with our true self. So doesn't the word *hypocrite* also describe a person who pretends to be less than he or she really is?

Harry Emerson Fosdick, pastor at Riverside Church in New York during the 1930s and 1940s, preached a sermon titled "On Seeming As Christian As You Are." Fosdick said that hypocrisy has two faces.

> You get it from two sides. Some people are hypocrites because they profess a Christian faith they are not living. Others are hypocrites because deep within themselves they have genuine Christianity they are not showing. Some hypocrites need to be told, be as good as you seem; other hypocrites need to be told, seem as good as you are (*The Power to See It Through,* 162).

Jerry Dunnam (Maxie's wife and Kimberly's mother), once attended a women's retreat led by a Roman Catholic nun, Sister Susan. A few days after returning from the retreat, Jerry received a letter from Sister Susan, which concluded with this prayer: "O God, help me to believe the truth about myself no matter how beautiful it is." Many of us need to pray this prayer. Though Christianity is the most affirming of all religions, for some it has elicited self-denial. To be sure, self-denial has its place but not for self-depreciation. We bear false witness when we lie to others by pretending to be something we are not, whether more than we are or less than we are.

We lie to ourselves when we try to transfer responsibility for our conduct on others or simply blame our action on circumstances. In the heat of fiery passion David had intercourse with Bathsheba, leading him to commit murder in order to save himself. He had Bathsheba's husband, Uriah, sent into battle in order that he might be killed. When word came back to him that Uriah was dead, he sought to take the blame off himself, saying to the messenger who had brought the word of Uriah's death, "Say this to Joab: 'Don't let this upset you; the sword devours one as well as another. Press the attack against the city and destroy it'" (2 Sam. 11:25, NIV).

Though we may think it impossible to act as deceitfully and destructively as David, we constantly need to examine ourselves. How often do we excuse our moral failures by blaming others for our conduct? allow ourselves to be controlled by circumstances? deceive ourselves into thinking we are not involved and can stay aloof from the social and moral structures in which we live?

Architect Albert Spear, Hitler's minister of armaments, deceived himself in order to avoid the guilt of seeing himself as a warmonger. Margaret Lewis Furse tells part of his story in her book *Nothing But the Truth? What It Takes to Be Honest.*

> After years of imprisonment for his war crimes, he arrived at a state (a state of grace it can be called in religious language) in which he knew he had nothing to lose by clarifying his self-reflections. He responded honestly to a letter from his daughter asking for an explanation of how an intelligent man like her father could go along with Hitler. Here is his answer in part:

> For me personally there was one factor making for the exclusion of all criticism, if I had wished to express any. You must realize that at the age of thirty-two, in my capacity as architect, I had the most splendid assignments of which I could dream. Hitler said to your mother one day that her husband could design buildings the like of which had not been seen for two thousand years. One would have had to be morally very stoical to reject the prospect. . . . More than once I have put to myself the question what I would have done if I had felt myself responsible for what Hitler did in other spheres of activity (the Holocaust and slave labor). Unfortunately, if I am to stay sincere, the answer would be negative. My position as an architect and the magnificent projects on which I was engaged became indispensable to me. I swallowed all the rest, never giving it a thought (Furse, *Nothing But the Truth?* 54–55).

Having removed himself from the political/military arena that was shaping the world of his time, Spear remained in self-reflective confusion in order to avoid guilt: "I did not see any moral ground outside the system where I should have taken my stand."

We lie to ourselves when we believe that we can do nothing in the face of latent evil or challenging opportunities. There is no form of good that we cannot make stronger, and there is no form of evil that we cannot in some measure weaken.

REFLECTING AND RECORDING

Examine your life to test the level of your deceitfulness in light of this truth: There is no form of good that we cannot make stronger, and there is no form of evil that we cannot in some measure weaken. In what ways are you guilty of telling yourself you can do nothing in the face of evil or challenging opportunity for good?

The psalmist prayed:

> O LORD, you have searched me and known me.
> You know when I sit down and when I rise up;
>   you discern my thoughts from far away (Ps. 139:1-2).

Write a prayer of confession, addressing the ways in which you may practice hypocrisy.

DURING THE DAY

Be attentive to ways you might oppose some evil that you observe and to ways you might help make some form of good stronger.

DAY 4
Sincerity—The Beginning of Honesty

> He also told this parable to some who trusted in themselves that they were righteous and regarded others with contempt. "Two men went up to the temple to pray, one a Pharisee and the other a tax collector. The Pharisee, standing by himself, was praying thus, 'God, I thank you that I am not like other people: thieves, rogues, adulterers, or even like this tax collector. I fast twice a week; I give a tenth of all my income.' But the tax collector, standing far off, would not even look up to heaven, but was beating his breast and saying, 'God, be merciful to me, a sinner!' I tell you, this man went down to his home justified rather than the other; for all who exalt themselves will be humbled, but all who humble themselves will be exalted."—Luke 18:9-14

Notice that Jesus directed this story "to some who trusted in themselves that they were righteous." Presumably the Pharisee possessed the virtues he claimed to have, confidently thanking God "that I am not like other people." The tax collector stood far off, not confident enough even to "look up to heaven." Though he doubted his own virtues, he somehow believed that in God's presence, he did not have to pretend to be other than he was.

To be sincere we have to trust that we do not have to pretend to be other than we are. Pretension is a lie and an enemy to God's intention for us. As the "members of one body," the church, we can grow only if we are real and honest with one another. Only as we open ourselves to other Christians can we find love, support, and encouragement. The Ephesians were warned, "Do not let any unwholesome talk come out of your mouths, but only what is helpful for building others up according to their needs, that it may benefit those who listen" (Eph. 4:29, NIV). Unwholesome talk can poison the atmosphere of relationships and of the church.

Humility, as well as trust, is required if sincerity is to be the beginning point of honesty. Humility is simply an awareness of who we really are, not a masochistic cowering of the self. The anonymous author of *The Cloud of Unknowing* said that the a person who is humble "becomes completely oblivious of himself, not worrying if he is wretched or holy" (Wolters, trans., *The Cloud of Unknowing*, 78).

The following story ties together the themes of humility, trust, and sincerity.

Kari Torjesen Malcolm served as a missionary to the Philippines for fifteen years after growing up in China as the daughter of missionaries. As a teenager, she was confined for a time during World War II in an internment camp, and there she discovered a deep truth that changed her life.

In the camp she was number sixteen, and only one of many Westerners who sought self-identity and comfort from others behind the walls and the electric fence that separated them from the outside world. There were other missionary kids in the same predicament, and often they managed to get together for a few moments of prayer—prayer for freedom.

But as time passed, Kari began to feel uneasy about these times of prayer. Freedom was becoming the ultimate goal in life, and God seemed to become less and less important—except for his answer to their prayers for freedom. She knew God was more than simply her ticket to freedom. She began to pray and search the Bible. "Gradually it dawned on me that there was just one thing the enemy could not take from me. They had bombed our home, killed my father, and put my mother, brothers and me into prison. But the one thing they could not touch was my relationship to my God."

Kari had a new outlook on life, and she no longer desired to join the others in their prayers for freedom. Her absence was immediately noticed, and she was confronted by her friend Debbie who rebuked her. "I cannot even remember trying to defend myself," Kari later recalled, "but Debbie must have surmised something of what had occurred in my thinking. Her reproof ended with the final taunt, 'So we aren't good enough for you anymore, eh? Getting holier than the rest of us, I can see.'"

It was a hard lesson for her; "As I walked away, I felt lonelier than I had ever felt in my life. My last bit of security was peeled off. This was the climax to the peeling process that had been going on through the war years with the loss of my father, my home, my education, my freedom. Now I no longer belonged to my peer group.

"It was only then that I was able to pray the prayer that changed my life; 'Lord, I am willing to stay in this prison for the rest of my life if only I may know You.' At that moment I was free" (Tucker, *Sacred Stories*, 29).

Humility makes no claims to integrity; it simply lives the truth and people recognize it.

REFLECTING AND RECORDING

Spend a few minutes pondering this question: How is my outer display of confidence in harmony with my inner awareness of my identity, especially my identity in relation to Christ?

Ephesians 4:15 (NIV) describes the Christian as one who in "speaking the truth in love, . . . will in all things grow up into . . . Christ." Briefly describe an experience during the past few months in which you hid the truth and called it love or someone acted thus in relation to you.

Briefly describe an experience during the past few months in which you hurt another with truthfulness that was not sincere love or in which someone hurt you in that way.

DURING THE DAY

Move through the day observant of pretension; seek to identify pretension in yourself and others.

DAY 5
Being a Truth

*I*n Herb Gardner's *A Thousand Clowns*, an uncle tells what he wants for his nephew:

> I just want him to stay with me till I can be sure he won't turn into a Norman Nothing. I want to be sure he'll know when he's chickening out on himself. . . . I want him to stay awake and know who the phonies are, I want him to know how to holler and put up an argument. I want a little guts to show before I let him go. I want to be sure he sees all the wild possibilities. . . . And I want him to know the subtle, sneaky, important reason he was born a human being and not a chair.—In Dunnam, *Be Your Whole Self*, 63

We can choose to chicken out on ourselves by playing a role—being a "Norman Nothing"—or to be a truth.

The New English Bible provides a meaningful translation of Matthew 16:26: "What will a man gain by winning the whole world, at the cost of his true self?" Within each of us a self yearns to be known and affirmed, to be cherished and developed to fulfillment. We are not to be hypocrites. Jesus himself did not escape the pressure of others' expectations. The Pharisees wanted him to be a pious legalist. The zealots cast him in the role of a militant revolutionist. His disciples sought to mold him into *their* kind of messiah. In an encounter between Jesus and his disciples, Jesus had asked, "Who do people say that the Son of Man is?" Peter responded, "You are the Messiah, the Son of the living God" (Matt. 16:13, 16). But even after that perceptive and marvelous affirmation, Peter could not let Jesus be himself. When Jesus began to tell his disciples that he had to go to Jerusalem and there suffer and die, it was Peter who objected: "God forbid. . . . This must never happen to you." With a sternness we often overlook in him, Jesus vigorously rebuked Peter, "Get behind me, Satan! You are a stumbling block to me" (Matt. 16:21-23).

Jesus would not allow himself to be cast in someone else's mold. He resisted the temptation to play a role or submit to the pressures of others' expectations because he had made prior commitments. He had established his priorities and loyalties. In this vivid story from the last week of Jesus' life, he gathers his disciples to celebrate the Passover in Jerusalem. As they assemble for that last meal, Jesus rises from the table. "Knowing . . . that he had come from God and was going to God . . . [Jesus] girded himself with a towel . . . and began to wash the disciples' feet" (John 13:3-5, RSV). Jesus' action that night was determined by the ultimate commitment of his life to God. His decision to come to Jerusalem in the first place was rooted in that commitment. Even in Gethsemane, where he later agonizes over the inevitable cross, his cry for deliverance is caught up in the ultimate commitment of his life: "Yet not what I will, but what thou wilt" (Mark 14:36, RSV).

When we cease playing a role and seek to be a truth, then our whole life—not just our words—will be committed to an authentic relationship with the Lord and a redemptive relationship with others.

REFLECTING AND RECORDING

Read the following passage slowly aloud:

> Now this I affirm and insist on in the Lord: you must no longer live as the Gentiles live, in the futility of their minds. They are darkened in their understanding, alienated from the life of God because of their ignorance and hardness of heart. They have lost all sensitivity and have abandoned themselves to licentiousness, greedy to practice every kind of impurity. That is not the way you learned Christ! For surely you have heard about him and were taught in him, as truth is in Jesus. You were taught to put away your former way of life, your old self, corrupt and deluded by its lusts, and to be renewed in the spirit of your minds, and to clothe yourselves with the new self, created according to the likeness of God in true righteousness and holiness.
>
> So then, putting away falsehood, let all of us speak the truth to our neighbors, for we are members of one another (Eph. 4:17-25).

Now read it again.

Stuart Briscoe reminds us that this passage describes three things that come our way (Briscoe, *The Ten Commandments*, 163 ff.).

Learning the truth. Spend some time reflecting on Jesus as the truth that is in marked contrast to the lying and deception characteristic of our world.

Loving the truth. When we learn God's truth we begin to love it and speak it in love. Where are you in loving the truth?

—⬳—

Living the truth. How does your lifestyle exhibit a person of honesty and integrity to others?

—⬳—

Write a brief prayer of commitment to these three dynamics: learning, loving, and living the truth.

DURING THE DAY

Pay close attention to occasions today when you slip into—or are tempted to slip into—playing a role rather than being a truth.

DAY 6
On These Depend the Whole Law and the Prophets

*M*artin Luther made the astonishing claim that "anyone who knows the Ten Command-ments perfectly knows the entire Scriptures." To "know" does not mean simply that we can recite these commandments, or that we know the content of them intellectually. If we *know* them by embodying them, then something revolutionary happens in our personal lives and in the corporate life of the church.

This embodiment hinges on the clarion note of the New Testament—love. "The glory that you have given me I have given them, so that they may be one, as we are one, I in them and you in me, that they may become completely one, so that the world may know that you have sent me and have loved them even as you have loved me" (John 17:22-23). "If I speak in the tongues of mortals and of angels, but do not have love, I am a noisy gong or a clanging cymbal" (1 Cor. 13:1). "Above all, clothe yourselves with love, which binds everything together in perfect har-mony" (Col. 3:14). "Support your faith with goodness, and goodness with knowledge, and knowledge with self-control, and self-control with endurance, and endurance with godliness, and godliness with mutual affection, and mutual affection with love" (2 Pet. 1:5-7).

> Beloved, let us love one another, because love is from God; everyone who loves is born of God and knows God.... Beloved, since God loved us so much, we also ought to love one another....

We love because he first loved us. Those who say, "I love God," and hate their brothers or sisters, are liars; for those who do not love a brother or sister whom they have seen, cannot love God whom they have not seen (1 John 4:7, 11, 19-20).

The whole Law and the Prophets depend on love. Romans 3:20 (NIV) tells us, "No one will be declared righteous in his sight by observing the law; rather, through the law we become conscious of sin." Seeking to keep the commandments makes us painfully aware that we simply cannot do it. Jesus told a young man who asked what he must do to inherit eternal life, "One thing you lack," he said. "Go, sell everything you have and give to the poor, and . . . come, follow me" (Mark 10:21, NIV). The young man was blind to the fact that in keeping the commandments from his youth, he probably had been breaking the tenth commandment—"you shall not covet."

The saving grace of Jesus Christ fills us with the power that enables us to focus on the foundation of commandment keeping: loving the Lord our God with all our hearts, minds, souls, and strength, and loving our neighbor as ourselves. Three practical suggestions will help us to begin appropriating the dynamic of love, the heart of the Christian faith.

First, have faith in love. On the cross Jesus staked everything on faith in the final victory of love. Somehow, "by main strength and awkwardness," as we say down in Perry County, Mississippi, we must have faith in love, believing it is the greatest power in the world, the throbbing heartbeat of God, the defining characteristic of Jesus, the dynamic of his life, death, and resurrection. We must believe that love overcomes all and is the positive expression of all the commandments.

Two, express love. With intentionality and discipline, we must learn to express love in all our relationships. To be sure, in our sinfulness, in our constantly falling short of the glory of God, to love is not always natural. Yet we have to discipline ourselves to express love in every situation.

Three, receive love. Receive first the love that Jesus constantly offers us. In John's Gospel Jesus stands at the door of our hearts, knocking. Christ is ready to bestow upon us all the grace of God's extravagant love poured out on humankind. Receive love not only from Christ but from others.

Benjamin West tells how he became a painter. One day his mother left him in charge of his little sister, Sally. He discovered some bottles of colored ink and began to paint Sally's portrait, leaving ink blots everywhere. When his mother returned home and saw the mess, grace—not anger and punishment—miraculously prevailed. Saying nothing, she picked up a piece of paper. She saw the drawing. "It's Sally!" she said immediately. Then she gave Benjamin a kiss. "My mother's kiss made me a painter," West later said (Dunnam, *Perceptions*, 94).

Love extravagantly given by God through God's Son, Jesus Christ, makes the kingdom come on earth as it is in heaven. When we have faith in that love, when we give it and receive it, the kingdom is demonstrated. This is the eternal love that defines the church, the people of God.

REFLECTING AND RECORDING

Recall and record here an experience of being loved that significantly affected your life.

Ponder what it means to "have faith in love."

———— ❦ ————

Ponder a situation you know or a relationship in which you are involved that could be changed for the better if love prevailed. Make some notes about why love is not being expressed, how it might be expressed, who needs to take initiative.

Recall a time or a period in your life when you realized you could not keep the commandments and live as Christ would have you live through your own power, with your own resources—that everything depended on grace, Christ's love of you. Reflect on that experience and your journey.

———— ❦ ————

DURING THE DAY

Express unconditional love to at least one person today. Find the occasion to witness to the power of love in your own life.

DAY 7
The Fellowship of Believers

*T*he church was born on the Day of Pentecost when the disciples were all together in one place. The Holy Spirit came dramatically to create the community of faith that was to be the fulfillment, the Christ-expression of the people of God that God had sought to shape throughout Old Testament days. Pentecost marked the entrance into the world of something not known before. Henceforth the church would confront every generation with the love of God, which "has been poured into our hearts through the Holy Spirit that has been given to us" (Rom. 5:5).

> They devoted themselves to the apostles' teaching and fellowship, to the breaking of bread and the prayers. Awe came upon everyone, because many wonders and signs were being done by the apostles. All who believed were together and had all things in common; they would sell their possessions and goods and distribute the proceeds to all, as any had need. Day by day, as they spent much time together in the temple, they broke bread at home and ate their food

with glad and generous hearts, praising God and having the goodwill of all the people. And day by day the Lord added to their number those who were being saved (Acts 2:42-47).

With a new reality of mutual love, under the power of the Holy Spirit, the church was born. This love is a unique expression of God's heart: "For God so loved the world, that he gave his only begotten Son" (John 3:16, KJV). The fruition and power of that love was seen on the cross as the Son of God suffered and died for humankind. This love of God in Christ led to Holy Spirit love being poured out at Pentecost on a love-filled community. This action fulfills God's intention for humankind, enabling us to live in community as those who are shaped by the law of God—including the Ten Commandments.

Those in the early love-filled church continually "devoted themselves to the apostles' teaching and to the fellowship, to the breaking of bread and to prayer" (Acts 2:42, NIV). The Word of God was not simply to be discussed among church members; it was to become the absolute authority for their lives. Wouldn't our attitude toward the Ten Commandments be altered if we saw them as the authority for our lives and if we knew we were a part of a fellowship that, in mutual support, would live out those commandments together?

The selfless fellowship of the first church resulted in dramatic action: Believers held everything in common; people sold their possessions and distributed the proceeds to anyone in need. They spent time together in the temple; they broke bread together in their homes. As the gospel spread and the church became more institutionalized, spending time together in homes shifted to weekly worship in the sanctuary. Yet the church building is not the place where God's activity is most vividly represented. The church exists not for itself but for the world.

A wonderful story about Marilyn Laslo illustrates not only the existence of the church for the world but the crucial place language has in God's kingdom enterprise. While Marilyn's missionary ministry in Papua New Guinea with Wycliffe Bible Translators was a beautiful example of missionary outreach, her ministry often encountered difficulties, especially in communicating cross-culturally. "Marilyn spent long days walking through the village pointing to objects that a villager would identify and copying down the phonetic sound of the words."

> Marilyn quickly discovered that learning a language involved far more than simply learning words. As she began to communicate with the people, she realized that "the center of life and seat of emotions was the *throat*. Thus, in the tribal tongue one would never say, 'I've asked Jesus to come into my *heart*,' but rather 'into my *throat*.' The more words she wrote down on her notebook, the more ignorant she realized she was. In her discouragement she often needed to be reminded why she was in Papua New Guinea.
>
> One day an old man asked her why she was carving with a thorn on a banana leaf (translated: *writing in her notebook*). She explained that she was learning the language so she could write God's Word on a banana leaf. "Incredulous" . . . the old man said, "You mean to say, Mama Marilyn, that God's talk and our talk can be carved on the banana leaf for us to see and understand?" Hardly believing what he was hearing, he shook his head and said, "Marilyn, oh, Marilyn, why did it take you so long to come?" (Tucker, *Sacred Stories*, 21).

REFLECTING AND RECORDING

The book of Acts describes the church as a vital fellowship, devoted to the apostles' teaching, prayer, and the breaking of bread together. This fellowship of believers lived not for itself but for others. In that kind of fellowship we can find the resources and accountability essential for living the Ten Commandments.

Reflect on your primary Christian fellowship in light of this understanding.

Write a prayer expressing your response to *The Workbook on the Ten Commandments* during these eight weeks.

DURING THE DAY

During the day and all coming days, seek to be a responsible part of Christian fellowship in order to find the resources and accountability essential for living the Ten Commandments.

Group Meeting for Week Eight

Leader: You will need a chalkboard or newsprint for this session.

INTRODUCTION

Today is the last meeting designed for this group. You have talked about the possibility of continuing to meet. Conclude those plans. Whatever you choose to do, determine the actual time line so that participants can make a clear commitment. Assign some persons to follow through with decisions that are made.

SHARING TOGETHER

Leader, save enough time for responses to question 12 about the full eight weeks.

1. Ask the group to refer to their Reflecting and Recording on Day 1 of this week where they listed ways we may bear false witness. List these on the chalkboard or newsprint until all are named.

2. Now ask, "Which of these have you been guilty of during the past three months?" Put a check (✓) by each one each time it is named.

3. Spend a few minutes talking about how responses compare with the traditional interpretation of this commandment.

4. Invite two or three persons to share their experience of being the victim of one of the following types of lying: (a) the destructive lie; (b) the defensive lie; (c) the defective lie; (d) the half-truth (Day 2).

5. Spend six to eight minutes discussing hypocrisy, paying attention to hypocrisy that
   • professes a Christian faith not lived.
   • hides a genuine Christian faith.
   What are the negative results of these forms of hypocrisy?

6. Continue six to eight minutes discussing hypocrisy, particularly such lying to ourselves as transferring responsibility for our conduct to others or blaming our actions on circumstances. Don't let extreme expressions of hypocrisy like addictive behavior distract the group from discussing everyday expressions of hypocrisy.

7. Take only three to five minutes to explore whether folks in your own community may be lying, telling themselves there is nothing they can do about situations of suffering and wrongdoing.

8. Invite a description of an experience in which someone is guilty of hiding the truth and calling it love (Day 4).

9. Invite someone to share an experience where one person destroyed another by truthfulness but called it love (Day 4).

10. Ask someone to read the prayer he or she wrote committing to the three dynamics of learning, loving, and living the truth (Day 5).

11. If you have four to five minutes, discuss what it means to be a truth rather than play a role.

12. Spend the remaining time sharing what these eight weeks have meant to individuals in the group—new insights, challenges, and disciplines they will work on.

PRAYING TOGETHER

Saint Teresa of Avila said the following about prayer:

> In prayer it is well to occupy ourselves sometimes in making acts of praise and love to God; in desires and resolutions to please Him in all things; in rejoicing at His goodness and that He is what He is; in desiring His honor and glory; in recommending ourselves to His mercy, and, at the same time, our own vileness and misery, and then to let Him give us what He pleases, whether it be showers or aridity; for He knows better than we what is most suitable for us (Order of Mercy, trans., *A Year with the Saints*, 266).

1. Spend two to three minutes in silence, thinking and praying for individuals about whom you are concerned and to whom you may need to speak.

2. Invite each group member to share a commitment he or she has made or prayer requests. As each person shares, have a time of prayer—silent or oral, preferably oral—so that each person will be prayed for specifically.

3. Ask two or three people to offer general prayers of thanksgiving for the eight-week experience and petitions for further growth and guidance.

4. A benediction is a blessing or greeting shared with another person or a group in parting. A variation on the traditional "passing of the peace" can serve as a benediction. The group forms a circle. The leader takes the hand of the person next to him or her, looks into his or her eyes, and says, "The peace of God be with you." That person responds, "And may God's peace be yours." Then that person takes the hand of the person next to him or her and says, "The peace of God be with you," and receives the response, "And may God's peace be yours." Continue passing the peace around the circle until everyone has had the opportunity to participate.

5. After the passing of the peace, speak to one another more spontaneously. Move around to different individuals in the group, saying whatever you feel is appropriate for your parting blessing to each person. Or simply embrace the person and say nothing. In your own unique way, bless each person who has shared this journey with you.

Sources

Barclay, William. *The Ten Commandments for Today*. San Francisco: Harper & Row, Publishers, 1983.

Briscoe, Stuart. *The Ten Commandments: Playing by the Rules*, rev. ed. Wheaton, Ill.: Harold Shaw Publishers, 1993.

Brueggemann, Walter. *Deuteronomy*, Abingdon Old Testament Commentaries. Nashville, Tenn.: Abingdon Press, 2001.

———. *Theology of the Old Testament: Testimony, Dispute, Advocacy*. Minneapolis: Fortress Press, 1997.

Cole, Darrell. "Can a War Be Just?" *Good News*, Nov./Dec., 2001.

Dawn, Marva J. *Keeping the Sabbath Wholly: Ceasing, Resting, Embracing, Feasting,* dedication. Grand Rapids, Mich.: William B. Eerdmans Publishing Co., 1989.

De Mello, Anthony. *Contact with God: Retreat Conferences.* Chicago: Loyola University Press, 1991. In Corinne Ware, *Saint Benedict on the Freeway* (see below).

Dunnam, Maxie. *Perceptions: Observations on Everyday Life*, vol. 2. Wilmore, Ky.: Bristol Books, 1991.

Dunnam, Maxie. *Be Your Whole Self.* Old Tappan, N.J.: Fleming H. Revell Co., 1970.

Eller, Vernard. *The* **MAD** *Morality, or the Ten Commandments Revisited*. Nashville, Tenn.: Abingdon Press, 1970.

Fosdick, Harry Emerson. *The Power to See It Through: Sermons on Christianity Today*. New York: Harper & Brothers, 1935.

Furse, Margaret Lewis. *Nothing But the Truth? What It Takes to Be Honest.* Nashville, Tenn.: Abingdon Press, 1981.

Gerber, Robin. "Why Turn Brilliant Lawyer into Barbie with Brains?" *USA Today*, February 11, 2002.

Hamilton, Adam. *Confronting the Controversies: A Christian Looks at the Tough Issues.* Nashville, Tenn.: Abingdon Press, 2001.

Hauerwas, Stanley and William Willimon. *The Truth About God: The Ten Commandments in Christian Life.* Nashville, Tenn.: Abingdon Press, 1999.

Ignatius. "Epistle of Ignatius to the Magnesians." In *Ante-Nicene Fathers*, vol. 1, *The Apostolic Fathers, Justin Martyr, Irenaeus.* Peabody, Mass.: Hendrickson Publishers, 1994.

Jones, Laurie Beth. *Jesus in Blue Jeans: A Practical Guide to Everyday Spirituality.* New York: Hyperion, 1997.

Kennedy, Gerald. *The Lion and the Lamb: Paradoxes of the Christian Faith.* New York: Abingdon Press, 1950.

Kipling, Rudyard. Quoted in "Timeless Tension," *Leadership: A Practical Journal for Church Leaders,* vol. 16, no. 4, Fall 1995.

Law, William. *The Works of the Reverend William Law*, vol. 7, *The Spirit of Prayer*. London: M. Richardson, 1749.

L'Engle, Madeleine with Carole F. Chase. *Glimpses of Grace: Daily Thoughts and Reflections.* San Francisco: HarperSanFrancisco, 1998.

Luccock, Halford E. *Like a Mighty Army: Selected Letters of Simeon Stylites.* New York: Oxford University Press, 1954.

Luther, Martin. *The Large Catechism of Martin Luther.* Translated by Robert H. Fischer. Philadelphia, Pa.: Muhlenberg Press, 1959.

Maxwell, John C. "Exodus," in *The Communicator's Commentary.* Edited by Lloyd J. Ogilvie. Vol. 5. Waco, Tex.: Word Books, 1987.

McDonald, Perry and William Odell. *Laws of Christian Living: The Commandments.* Huntington, Indiana: Our Sunday Visitor, Inc., 1986.

Meyer, F. B. *Devotional Commentary on Exodus.* Grand Rapids, Mich.: Kregel Publications, 1978.

Meyers, T. Cecil. *Thunder on the Mountain.* Nashville, Tenn.: Abingdon Press, 1965.

Miller, Calvin. "Gradual Brimstone." Preaching Today audiotape 214. Carol Stream, Ill.: Christianity Today International (ChristianityToday.com).

Order of Mercy/Mount Saint Joseph's Seminary, trans. *A Year with the Saints.* Rockford, Ill.: Tan Books and Publishers, Inc., 1891, 1972.

Redpath, Allen. *Law and Liberty.* London and Glasgow: Pickering and Inglis, 1981.

Raz, Sincha. *Hasidic Wisdom: Sayings from the Jewish Sages.* Northvale, N.J.: Jason Aronson, 1997. In Corinne Ware, *Saint Benedict on the Freeway* (see below).

Stone, Lawson G. "What Does It Really Mean to Take the Lord's Name in Vain?" *Decision* (March 2000).

Tolstoy, Leo. "Father Sergius" at www.classicreader.com/read.php/sid.1/bookid.328/sec.6/

Tucker, Ruth A. *Sacred Stories: Daily Devotions from the Family of God.* Grand Rapids, Mich.: Zondervan Publishing House, 1989.

United Methodist Hymnal, The. Nashville, Tenn.: The United Methodist Publishing House, 1989.

Vanauken, Sheldon. "The Loves," *Under the Mercy.* In Chuck Colson, "Why Christians Divorce: The Sanction of Eros." *BreakPoint* 2/17/00, PreachingToday.com 2/09/02.

Ware, Corinne. *Saint Benedict on the Freeway: A Rule of Life for the 21st Century.* Nashville, Tenn.: Abingdon Press, 2001.

Wesley, John. *The Works of John Wesley.* Grand Rapids, Mich.: Zondervan Publishing House, n.d.

Wolters, Clifton, trans. *The Cloud of Unknowing and Other Works.* Baltimore: Penguin Books, 1978.

www.PreachingToday.com (in association with ChristianityToday.com)

Affirmation Cards

> *God is everywhere,*
> *but to find God anywhere,*
> *we must meet God somewhere.*

O LORD, you have searched me and known me.
You know when I sit down and when I rise up;
    you discern my thoughts from far away.
You search out my path and my lying down,
    and are acquainted with all my ways.
Even before a word is on my tongue,
    O LORD, you know it completely.
You hem me in, behind and before,
    and lay your hand upon me.
Such knowledge is too wonderful for me;
    it is so high that I cannot attain it.

                              —Psalm 139:1-6

THE TEN COMMANDMENTS

You shall have no other gods before me.

You shall not make for yourself an idol.

You shall not take the name of the Lord your God in vain.

Remember the sabbath day and keep it holy.

Honor your father and mother.

You shall not murder.

You shall not commit adultery.

You shall not steal.

You shall not bear false witness.

You shall not covet.